ANAHID GOR

Goodbye Istanbul !

Published by: Providence Publications
52 Cottesmore Court
Kelso Place
London
W8 5QL

First published: 2003

ISBN: 0-9546887-0-8

Printed by:
ProPrint
Riverside Cottages
Old Great North Road
Stibbington
Cambs. PE8 6LR

Dedication

I dedicate this book to the memories of my beloved husband, Krikor, and my dear brother, Diran, and to my three precious daughters, without whose help and encouragement I would not have been able to accomplish my dream and see my life story in print

Anahid

Krikor

INTRODUCTION

When I began writing my story as to how and why I came to England, I only meant to write a short essay, without going into details, just to show it is possible to become an asylum seeker, quite unintentionally. Once started, I had to mention the hostels, the schools, my brother, my conditions at home, and how it became possible for me to adapt to new ways of life so different from the old.

A little red book given to me was my incentive and my inspiration. It is called, "Memoirs of a bloody foreigner in pidgin English", by Elahé, a young Iranian girl, a friend of my daughter. So I decided, after much thought, to give it a try and see how I would persevere. I never dreamt I would go this far. The more I probed into my past, the more I discovered down memory lane, freewheeling deeper and deeper into it, remembering more and more; it was like getting sucked into quick-sand. I couldn't bring the book to a close without recounting the circumstances that led me to London this time for good.

Going back to the time when Krikor and I had just met, neither of us had the slightest idea that our destiny was already decided. He was a bachelor, a confirmed bachelor, shy and withdrawn, living alone without any definite plans. I was waiting here in transit, to go to America to join my brother. I was also alone, living and sharing accommodation with other girls. It so happened that our paths crossed and we met as if it was planned. It was meant to be. We have a very apt word in Armenian for this situation, we call it "djagadakir" – "letters written on your forehead" – which means your fate.

As time went by, we passed the "bachelor/single girl, freedom, do as you like, have fun" times. Our relationship became serious. We started married life with open eyes, resolved to keep our vows until death do us part. We would stay together thirty years, never separated, day and night, till death did us part so cruelly.

After losing my dear husband, my life had a big void. I tried to fill that vacuum with activities that I had been involved with before, now with even more zest. Soon there was no longer a gap to fill or an idle corner. I was altogether committed to community affairs, like the AGBU, the Church Council, and especially the Armenian House.

While writing about my past memories, I wandered into spiritual and other subjects that frequently occupied my thoughts. The result is this book. I completed my first draft in the New Year of 2003, and have spent recent months revising my draft and having it edited and reviewed. I would like to extend heartfelt gratitude to Mr Garbis Yessayan and Mr Haig Abadjian for kindly reviewing my book.

Since starting this book, I have had the misfortune of losing my brother, Diran. I would like to think he would have enjoyed reading this book – and hope you do too.

ANAHID GORGODIAN
London, August 2003

10-12-04

Dear Pat,

Remember me from old Kenilworth? I always remember the old Times and I am so grateful for your friendship and support during the three unforgettable years when we were so young and inexperienced.

I got your address from June, I hope it's correct.

This is my life story, Hard work, I hope you enjoy it.

Merry Christmas and a HAPPY NEW YEAR—

love,

Anahid.

CHAPTER 1 NEW BEGINNINGS

The year is 1946; it is late September, and I am about to leave my birthplace, my parents, relatives, friends and neighbours, to board a plane to London. I do not really want to embark on this adventure. I cannot speak English, I don't know much about England and to make matters worse, some people put me off by saying I'll be "eating boiled cabbage every day" - which I hate anyway.

A crowd of about 25 people have come to see me off at Istanbul Airport. There are no restrictions, no checking whatsoever, they are all gathered right up to the door of the aircraft, carefree and unsupervised. We are being photographed, on such a memorable occasion, me on the steps of the plane, lost behind a bouquet of gladiolas given to me by the editor of the daily newspaper where I had been a columnist for a few years.

Farewell to friends and family
at the steps of the plane

I am Armenian. I was born in Istanbul, educated first at Armenian and then French High Schools, subsequently finding office work as a secretary-clerk. While I am resigned to my situation, despite the fact that nothing exciting ever happens in my life, why am I then suddenly alarmed at the prospect of this major change? I am going towards the unknown, leaving behind my poor parents, which is especially hard when I am their sole provider. They are not sick or invalid, but all the same, a pathetic ageing couple, father unemployed, mother wretched with worry. Amazingly, she is the one who urges me to go. She persuades me to get out of this rut and follow my destiny towards better and good things, or so she hopes.

The crowd surrounding me is laughing and joking, wishing me luck, and some envying me, I imagine, for this daring adventure. In those days, travelling abroad by air was rare. "Write to me!", "Have a good trip!". At last, the time has come for the final goodbyes. Hugging, kissing, crying. My father looks helpless, my mother cannot open her tearful eyes. "I love you", I cry and run up the steps that are pulled in after me. The door is firmly shut by the stewardess and I am shown to my seat by the window.

They are still out there, my people, waving and shouting "bon voyage!". Eventually they are guided away to the Airport building, while my carriage starts rumbling, showing signs of movement. Gradually the aircraft makes a half circle on the runway slowly gathering speed, then off it goes, leaving the ground and soaring into the air. Automatically, I am clenching the arm-rests. I am not really afraid of flying, this is just instinct. It never occurs to me that flying can be dangerous. In those days, you didn't hear of plane accidents, they were not commonplace. Ignorance is bliss. We are off, up and up. And everything down there is melting away under the clouds. I shut my eyes as nothing is visible below us, but I can still visualise the scene in my mind's eye, everyone who came to see me off, and I carried that picture with me for a long time ...

*   *   *   *

It all started when my only sibling and elder brother, who lived in Paris for 14 years, arranged this journey for me, bought my ticket and enrolled me at a college in Manchester, England. When Diran first suggested this idea, I rejected it outright. No and no again! How could I leave our parents who were so dependent on me? And why England? If anywhere at all, I would rather go to Paris. At least I could speak the language, and later maybe our parents could come too. But, no: my dear brother explained to me that he himself had no prospects in Europe, and intended to try his luck in America, the land of opportunity, hopefully very soon. He said in his letter, "if you don't accept this offer now, I may not be in a position to help you for a long time".

This was in 1946, not very long after the war. They were hard times of uncertainty, of unemployment for many people. Diran was very much aware that I had been holding the fort while he finished his education: first in Venice, then in Paris and Toulouse. While my brother was pursuing his career and getting degree after degree, my only consolation was that, one day soon, we would all go to Paris, where he would be doing well, and we would all be safe and secure without financial worries. Castles in the air, maybe. It never occurred to me to resent my situation. In those days, you didn't leave home and go your own way. You stayed with your family until you married. In the circumstances, it was taken for granted that I should be the bread-winner. A responsibility was thrust upon me and that was that. My father was jobless, I couldn't walk out on my beloved parents, who were

3

unlucky and helpless. Anyway, where would I go? And how? They needed me, I needed them.

Even though I was not happy in my job, I dared not walk out. My boss knew of my desperation and he exploited me. I was doing three different things at the same time: typing, being a cashier and writing the invoices by hand. No holidays were allowed, paid or unpaid; no sick leave, no absences. Just ten hours of responsible, hard work every day, six days a week. I had only Sundays in which to fit in all my personal activities.

The Galata Bridge in Istanbul

We lived in a small flat in an old house, with no hot water and no mod cons, but it was what we could afford. We economised on everything. I worked in the city, and I would walk to and from the office in all weathers to save the fare. It was a long way. Crossing the Galata Bridge twice daily was a punishing exercise in winter, while the sea underneath it was raging with angry waves, the wind blowing fiercely from all directions, turning your umbrella inside out and threatening to lift you into the air like Mary Poppins. Or the snow blizzards would blind your eyes, freeze your fingers even through woollen gloves; and if your coat wasn't thick enough or your shoes let the water in, then you'd get chilblains. You would just be prey to the elements. There would be no time to feel sorry for yourself, it was a way of life. You get serious winter in Istanbul, three months solid, without a break. At least you know what to expect. But I was young and, as I said, I had hopes and dreams, things to look forward to. My brilliant brother would be our saviour, getting us out of this hell.

My mother was so proud of her son, she used to boast about him. Her son was "a mathematician, an electrical engineer, a genius, he had inventions". Whereas, I felt I was a failure. I had no degree, I couldn't afford to go to university. Most of my school friends did, even those who were far behind me in most subjects.

I discovered I could write. I started by writing freelance, in the newspaper on social subjects. Then I did some translations and produced short stories, where I would express my frustrations and inner feelings by making my heroine disadvantaged in some way. Disillusioned, she would live a hard life in an unjust world, she would struggle to keep going, and eventually she would meet her gallant prince and all would be well. Typical!

When I re-read those stories now, I find them very innocent, naive and simplistic. But my readers liked them. My pen-name was Diana which is my real name, Anahid, read backwards. I had to use a pen-name as I did not want my identity to be known. I was using many of the people I knew in my stories, and had found a welcome outlet for achievement that did not require a university degree.

Once I started putting pen to paper, I couldn't stop and the newspaper was just as eager to publish any material I gave them. I even tried writing poetry when I felt very emotional, but it wasn't my forté. But I was very audacious on controversial social subjects. Often, feedback would come from the rival paper criticising me. And funnily enough, when the bad press was from well-known and established writers, I used to get quite a kick out of it. They were taking notice of me, those big heads! And needled, I used to give as good as I got. My pen was now confident enough to fight back and my paper encouraged me. This controversy was selling well on both sides. The critics suggested that this intrepid columnist must be a man disguised behind a feminine pseudonym. My pen was quite famous by now, and I was rather enjoying this game.

In 1942, I wrote an article under the heading "Why the Armenians don't have their own tango music". It was rather a lengthy piece. I argued that we shouldn't be dancing to the tune of Greek tangos which had inundated the market, when we had so many talented musicians ourselves. Couldn't anyone in our community compose a couple of tangos? This generated such a furore in the rival paper, that I was showered with a crescendo of abusive words. On the other hand, a gallant musical supporter was so touched by my challenge, that he immediately composed two tangos, called "Dream" and "I loved you" and dedicated them to me. And while they were being played live for the first time at a formal tea-dance, the sheet music was maliciously snatched from the conductor's tripod and was quickly whisked away. Fortunately, it was not the original copy.

Both papers were now full of the tango stories. Amazingly, a new trend had just started. I was congratulated by so many people writing supportive articles and praising me for my just observations, that the editors of my paper, "Jamanak", couldn't publish any more. They declared "if we give space to all of them, there will be no room in our paper to print anything else!" So they handed me a pile of unpublished manuscripts of congratulations from sympathisers that I still keep and occasionally re-read to remind me of that bright idea of mine, that initiative, which I wonder if anybody remembers now, unless they happen to be my contemporaries back in Istanbul.

Following all that, even in other Armenian communities in the Near East, very tuneful, lovely Armenian tangos suddenly came on the scene. I had started a vogue that would give incentive to budding composers who produced many beautiful dance tunes which have been played everywhere since then.

This fantasy world of writing was my outlet that kept me going. Now that I was established, my brother was coming to upset my lifestyle. One day, he declared he had made a new revolutionary invention for printing patterns on textile materials. On enquiring, he was told that the best place to sell it was Manchester, Europe's textile capital. So, off he went by train and ship; without even speaking the language or knowing anyone there, he managed to find the right people who would be interested in his discovery.

My brother did not lack moral courage, he was a fighter. He sold his new invention for £600. At the time, the sum was a small fortune, which he decided to use in bringing me to England to learn English, so that later on, I could follow him to America. His plan for himself was daring, to say the least, but the one for me was even more so. My one way ticket from Istanbul was originally for a flight via Cairo where I would change planes, as there was no direct route to London in those days. But when it was time to collect my ticket, the agent told me that there was a new service flying BOAC which was direct and avoided the need to change planes. Of course, I jumped at the option, it would be cheaper too. The difference would be payable in Manchester where originally the ticket was bought.

The supposedly direct journey on that inaugural flight lasted three days. The first night was spent in Athens in Hotel Grande Bretagne - very posh. The next day, we had a stop-over at Rome Airport for refuelling. The second night we stayed in Marseille's Hotel Splendide, another luxury hotel with a big double bedroom that was lavishly furnished - I had only seen the like in Hollywood films. Then, in the morning, we were off again, at long last headed for England's London Airport.

This was a whirlwind adventure that I could not have imagined in my wildest dreams. So far so good, and I was now getting excited. I was so looking forward to meeting my brother again after 14 years! From the plane, we were all escorted to the waiting BOAC Airport Bus which drove to the terminus in Victoria. I was animated and raring to go. But since I could not understand the announcements on the loudspeaker, I naturally followed everyone else: from plane to the bus, then arriving at the terminus, I followed the other passengers. As people were piling into the waiting taxis, I copied them when it was my turn in the queue. Thus, I and my luggage went into a taxi, and I waited to be taken to the next stage of my journey where my brother would be waiting to welcome me.

Or so I thought! The poor inexperienced girl that I was, was startled when the driver, until then patiently waiting for my orders, stretched his neck towards the back of the cab, irritated, and called "where are you going?". I could understand that much from my short course at evening classes. Helplessly bewildered, I replied, "I don't know". The driver was not amused since I was now the last person in the queue and he had lost a real customer. Angrily, he shouted: "Get out!"

CHAPTER 2   OFF TO MANCHESTER

Furiously, the taxi-driver took my case and dumped it on the pavement. I got out in disgrace, in despair, in shame. What now? Thrown out on the pavement with my luggage, tears rolling down my face, I went back inside the terminus. Looking through the crowds, with all its comings and goings, loudspeakers blaring, I couldn't see my brother anywhere. Desperate, and lost in that new world of strangers, I cursed myself for leaving my small and intimate world. I had no English money, I couldn't speak the language and there was no one to help me. People passed by without even glancing at me, as I sat in a corner waiting for a miracle to happen.

I couldn't understand why my brother hadn't come to meet me. I couldn't walk around carrying my suitcase, as it was heavy, nor could I leave it unattended. Anyway, I didn't know where to go! In this new world, everything seemed hostile. I was hungry, thirsty, and extremely anxious, thinking there must be a terrible mistake somewhere. Maybe Diran had got the dates mixed up - but, if so, what was I to do next?

I was lost in a chaotic airline terminus where people were buzzing around confidently while I was facing a big dark canyon ready to swallow me up. I felt sick. Miserably, I started looking around for inspiration. Then, I noticed a uniformed girl at a desk, talking sweetly to whoever went up to her. Would I dare? What should I say, and how? I was a 26 year old woman - I could hardly act as a little lost girl crying for Mummy! But with the unexpected absence of my brother to greet me, coupled by lack of know-how and the language barrier, my insecurities had come to a head.

The impact of culture shock was much more acute than it now seems in retrospect. I gathered my courage and approached the desk. The assistant asked how she could help me, and when I replied that I spoke French, she smiled and asked me to wait. A little later, a man in uniform came to meet me. He explained in English that if I spoke in French, he would understand. I told him that I had just arrived and had nobody to meet me. I said also that my ticket cost less than originally paid, and could they, please, on account, send a telegram to my brother. I had no telephone number for him. Luckily, they agreed to do this.

Some time later, there was an envelope delivered to my name by courier. Diran was unable to come, but had sent enough money for a taxi and train ticket to Manchester. The nice girl and the messenger kindly put me in a taxi, and asked the driver to see me settled on the right train, which he did. They were not so bad, those English people, after all. I was very thankful. I kept repeating, "Merci, merci beaucoup."

So now, at last, I was heading towards my destination. Presently, I would suffer from sleep, hunger, thirst, and worst of all, I needed the toilet. Was there a toilet on the train, and how could I leave my case? That pathetic old case that contained nothing precious but all my worldly possessions. I couldn't risk losing it, and coming from a country where every hazard was possible, I was suspicious of everybody. I just sat tight.

The train left London. Each time it stopped after long stretches, now and then, I would jump up and ask "Manchester?". "No" they would say, "not yet, there is plenty of time". It felt like an eternity. By now, my ears were getting used to English words and knowing French was a great help. Not much more left, I hoped. I was definitely going to meet my brother, and everything would be OK.

I would forget my miserable existence, my dead-end job, that allowed us just about to survive. I remembered how afraid I used to be of getting ill and being absent in case they replaced me straight away. From now on, unemployment, deprivation, insecurity would be things of the past. In this far corner of the world, where people were civilised and rich, and lived in decent accommodation, would I adapt and be like them? Would I be able to go to the doctor if I became ill, or to the dentist if I had toothache? Where I came from, there were no benefits of any kind, no welfare system, nothing free. I remembered my poor mother drinking boiled water to get better after an attack of flu. We did not even possess any aspirins. And I also remembered how I had pulled out my own bad tooth and gargled with salt water for the blood to stop. We could afford nothing but just the bare essentials, and learned to get better with home remedies. Thank goodness nothing serious happened.

At last, the train stopped with a loud jerk. Passengers jumped up from their seats, collecting their belongings. I picked up my own pathetic case and struggled out of the train. The platform was unlit, and there was no one waiting except for one solitary shadow that I likened to my brother. It was him indeed. I hadn't seen him for 14 years. In my joy and relief, I even forgot to ask why he hadn't met me earlier. Now, no more indecision. I was in his hands and he was in charge.

I spent my first night in England on a folding bed in the lounge of the YWCA Central in St Peter Street, Manchester, where they kindly made an exception to their rules and took me in after midnight. Then, Diran arranged for me to stay at their residential branch in Whalley Range, where eventually I would live the next three years. At the time, all this seemed an unbelievable development. When he left me at that large house, full of girls noisily going about their daily lives, I felt completely out of place. As if I was in a very bad dream, and I would wake up and find myself back where I belonged, with familiar faces and places.

Presently, I was shown to a bed in the corner of a large room that I would share with three others. I sat on my bed not knowing what to do next. I looked around: four beds, one in each corner, with a side table and a green felt curtain behind which to hang our clothes, a chest of four drawers - one drawer for each of us - and a wash basin. The other girls were going in and out without taking much notice of me. They were not very friendly at first, as probably my own attitude wasn't very encouraging. I was very much a foreigner, which they were not used to seeing in those days.

Gradually, the ice broke, and I was told the rules. In the office, I was given a ration book and the Warden kept the food coupons. She explained that I was there for bed, breakfast and evening meals, with full board at weekends, breakfast at 8am sharp and supper at 6pm. Everybody was out during the day, to college, university or to work. I was shown the stop where to take my bus, a big, red, double decker that was new to me, to go to my college, The High School of Commerce, and was told where to get off at the other end.

I had been enrolled by my brother to attend a special course for foreign students in Business Economics, combined with Geography and History. All the other students on the course had a reasonable if not good knowledge of English, whereas mine was elementary. My French became very useful in understanding the text books or anything written, but it took me at least a fortnight to be able to follow the lectures. I made friends with the only French girl there, Françoise. There were two other girls who were Dutch, and the rest were all young men - Danish, Dutch and one Tunisian. Eventually, I fitted in quite well but not before getting bad marks for my homework.

It took me some time to find my feet and get into the swing of things, both at college and at the hostel. Hearing this new language all the time felt like force-feeding. My brother had gone back to Paris with a promise of returning soon. Letters from home were such a relief, they were my only relaxation. I used to grab my mail and run for the bus, reading it on my way to college.

The same conductor everyday used to greet me with "good morning love", which I found very indecent. How dare he call me "love"? When I told the girls at the hostel how indignant I was, they reassured me that it was quite a normal greeting. You would be called "love" everywhere, and it didn't mean anything offensive. Many more things I had to learn, and to accept in this new way of life. It was more than a culture shock, it would be a complete make-over, inside-out. I would have to change my own habits and ideas on things. My transformation was gathering speed. I still read my mail on the bus, and the conductor still called me "love" with other occasional remarks, such as "does he still love you, dear?". He probably thought all my letters were from the same person.

At the hostel, I was the only one receiving mail from abroad. Sometimes, it felt as if I was living in two different worlds. Nevertheless, I was changing all the time. Not only was I getting better at communicating but also adapting to English ways and habits. Breakfast was the most unusual meal for me. Having cereal with cold, unboiled milk in the morning was new; also, eating meat and fish in the form of bacon and kippers, which I had never tasted before. I began to enjoy them. I used to have lunch at the college canteen, which was nothing spectacular, but edible and adequate for one shilling and a penny. There would be supper back at the hostel at 6pm. Again, this involved unusual dishes for me, such as rissoles, corned beef, steak and kidney pie or shepherds pie, liver and onions, all with mashed potatoes and either boiled cabbage or tinned peas and carrots. I had never had a big appetite before at home, and my mother worried that being such a fussy eater by nature, I would now skip meals and be malnourished. The opposite happened. Whether it was the change of environment or company, I don't know: but suddenly my appetite improved. There was little I could not eat, apart from black pudding and cheese and onion pie (I had never tolerated cheese before). The desserts were most acceptable. We never ate puddings at home, we finished every meal with fruit. Here, fruit was scarce. We had the occasional apple or banana as a treat.

The only ration coupons we were allowed to keep were for things we bought for ourselves, such as soap, sweets and clothes. I had never heard of shampoo before and still used soap to wash my hair and my clothes by hand.

Time was passing very quickly. I had already been in Manchester for over a month when suddenly there was commotion and excitement in the House. Everybody was speaking about Guy Fox and the party they were planning for him. I had never heard of that name before, and thought he was someone who was going to visit us. When I asked if he was young, I was stared at in amazement: "Don't you know who Guy Fawkes is? He is dead, he tried to burn down the Houses of Parliament ..." Now it was my turn to be amazed. "If he was so bad, why are you going to have a party for him?" The girls were surprised that I was so ignorant about such an important time in their history. There were many other things I would get to learn or become accustomed to.

Presently, we were preparing for the party which was to be held in the gardens surrounding the house. The girls explained that there was going to be a bonfire where they would burn an effigy of Guy Fawkes and also cook sausages and chestnuts. There was some organising to do. The boys from the YMCA were invited, and boyfriends too. My brother was back again so I invited him to join us. After the bonfire and food, they moved all the chairs in the dining room to create space for dancing. We had a gramophone and a few records. Most girls had boyfriends or found a partner from the YMCA. The DOMSCI girls were very popular - they were the Domestic Science students - very lively, forward and street-wise.

My brother asked me to introduce my room-mates to him. Two of them had already found partners, there was only Gladys who was a wallflower like me. She was rather plain and a little shy. My brother asked her to dance with him, and she was absolutely delighted. Fortunately, I wasn't left alone for very long. I had a handsome Danish boy who partnered me the whole evening. He was quite charming. His English wasn't any better than mine, so we got on very well.

Then, the inevitable happened, he asked me out the next day. The girls warned me about him. They said that "Great Danes were dangerous" and they didn't mean the dogs either. They were right, he did not want to be "just good friends", so I put an end to it. As to Gladys, she was so taken by my brother, she said there was only one gentleman that night and that was him. I know full well that his intentions were not entirely unselfish, he was trying to secure some support for me.

When my brother left for the USA, I had to become more independent. Though at first, it felt like being abandoned in a ship under the command of a captain with strict rules: no noise, lights out after ten, and everyone had to be in by then as the front door was locked. I had no problem with all that, but some of the DOMSCI girls would often return late from a night out, and their confidantes would leave one sash window in the ground floor lounge slightly open from the bottom, so that it could be pushed up and they could jump in.

Those girls were full of life. At weekends, you could hear them singing all the pop songs of the time, and as I like singing very much, I would join in the sing-songs. I remember, the most popular tunes were: "I like to take you on a slow boat to China", "What's behind the green door?", "I don't want her, you can have her, she's too fat for me", "Open the door, Richard", "East is east, and west is west, and the wrong one I have chose", "Money is the root of all evil", "One day I'm gonna write the story of my life", "Give me five minutes more only five minutes more".

There was a pianola in the dining room which was used mostly by Pat, the music student. For the rest of us, it was like a toy. Using the foot pedals, we could play ready-made music and some well-known tunes, like "The Sheikh of Araby, your heart belongs to me" or the "Toreador" from Carmen.

I enjoyed the youthful company of the girls. I was now accepted even though I couldn't rock and roll or jive like them; I was used to ballroom dancing and they were not. I was also getting used to the English diet and new social ways. In short, I was settling down rather well. The YWCA was like a social boarding school, where not only did I learn spoken English steadily (I had some thirty teachers) but also, their company made me feel young and fancy-free. The letters I got from friends were getting less and less as I was losing touch with them.

Only the ones from my parents never stopped and unfortunately became more and more depressing. My parents were lost without me, even though my father was trying harder to get odd jobs that would keep them going for a while. We were all hoping that my brother would soon do well in America, and we would be saved from this insecure situation.

In my spare time, I sent correspondence to "Jamanak", the Armenian newspaper in Istanbul, now using my real name. I sent them articles about living in England and the English people. Life here was so unlike my old existence in Istanbul. The culture shock was still with me, though gradually becoming less, and I used to write in my columns all kinds of things that would seem unusual, odd and interesting to them back home.

For instance, the terrible smog in Manchester in the winter of 1947 that lasted for days and paralysed the city. Also, left-handedness: it was so scarce in Istanbul that it was considered a defect or sign of weakness. If a mother saw that tendency in her child, she would try to discourage the trait and correct it by forcing the use of the right hand. You hardly saw left-handed people in Istanbul. They were called "cholak" in Turkish, not a complimentary word, meaning something like "clumsy".

Soon it was Christmas. To me, this first holiday was a big novelty. We Armenians do not celebrate our Christmas on December 25th, but on January 6th. My only memory of Noël is at the French school in Istanbul, and I remember going to the midnight mass in the school chapel, where those wonderful "Sisters of

Mercy" with their huge white starched head-dresses and long blue gowns would teach us catechism.

I loved and respected those amazing selfless women, who abandoned normal life - of love and family, possessions, fun, small luxuries and friends - to spend their life instead in prayer and teaching. Soeur Marie was my form-mistress, kindness itself, and she also taught us maths and science with immense patience; Soeur Cécile, short and ugly, but so loveable, she taught us classical literature with devotion. Soeur Marthe, arts and crafts teacher, very good looking; Soeur Louise, a bit stiff and serious, but you could tell she was suffering, either physical or emotional pain. The girls whispered that she was a princess with a tragic past.

The school was called Sainte Pulchérie, and was not far from where I lived. After graduating from "Essayan", the Armenian High School for girls, my brother wanted me to improve my spoken French by going to a French school in preparation for a university course in Paris. This had always been my dream; as it turned out, a dream that wasn't meant to be. Nevertheless, I always thought French was a beautiful language.

Coming back to my first Christmas in Manchester, I was surprised to see most of the girls packing their bags to go Home. At the time, it seemed odd that students should live away from home, rather than with their parents. But my first Christmas in England is very memorable to me, mainly because for the first time, I heard English carols. The one that took my breath away was Silent Night. To this day, every Christmas time, when I hear it I am spellbound and relive those nostalgic days back in December 1946, when the carol reduced me to tears and does still.

19

In the New Year of 1947, after the holidays, I went back to College for the second term. I was now enjoying the course even though I wasn't sure where it would lead me. My brother had arranged it as an excuse to bring me over to England. In a few months, the course would end. Diran was making preparations to go to America and stay with cousins. There was still some money in the Bank for me to live on, but what I didn't realise was that when the money ran out, I would be on my own.

Before he left, still as hopeful as ever, Diran said it wouldn't be long before he would sell one of his new inventions, and reassured me that everything would be OK. He enrolled me in at a Secretarial College, "The Loreburn", so that in the meantime, when I qualified, I could earn a living. But then, neither of us realised that according to the inscription in my passport, I was "Not allowed work of any kind, paid or unpaid". We had not taken any notice of that very important restriction.

Hardly one course was over at the High School of Commerce, when I started the secretarial course at Loreburn College. It was very embarrassing for me, as I was in a class with young teenage school-leavers, and I was at least ten years older. Also, whereas previously, I was with adult graduates from abroad, now I was the only foreigner. Those girls were probably not interested in higher education or couldn't afford it. My name was unrecognisable and certainly unpronounceable by them. I was very much the odd one out. I tried to keep myself to myself so that no one asked me any questions. Those spotty, giggly girls looked down on me because I was so different from them. My brother tried to dismiss my concerns, "they'll soon give up, don't worry" he said.

After a week or so, only one very shy girl tried to talk to me. She wanted to know how old I was. Unprepared, but thinking quickly, I said "Twenty". I was lying, of course, instinctively aware that my true age would have placed a huge age gap between us. I was surprised when she said, smiling sweetly, "You don't look it, you know" and I knew she meant it. Thank God - that was one problem solved.

She continued, "I told my parents there is a French girl in our class, and they want you to come and have tea with us on Sunday. Can you come?" I was flattered. She gave me their address and told me how to get there.

I was glad to be accepted at last by someone. Why was it that they thought I was French? Perhaps because my brother came from Paris and spoke in French, or maybe because I never denied it either. I was not ashamed of being Armenian, only no-one would have even heard of the word and I didn't want to start explaining. In those days, people didn't travel much and only the very educated knew about far away countries. So, I went to their house and was careful to be on time. In England, when people say four o'clock, they mean just that. I was becoming European!

I did like that unpretentious and modest family and felt quite at ease. They doted on their daughter and it was their wish that she would start working as soon as she finished the secretarial course. They wanted her to be independent. I could see that in England, it was very important to be "independent". That word was not in my vocabulary. These good, honest people, a loving family, with a cosy little house, they were trying to secure their daughter's future. I had a very pleasant day with them, and was relieved they didn't ask too many questions. I was thankful for their consideration, and thought they were charming.

I had a friend now in class, and was not isolated anymore. During breaks, we used to talk about the course or what it would be like to work in an office. She couldn't wait to start earning her own living, even though she would still live at home.

All the girls I met wanted to be independent. No one, like me, expected her brother to secure her future. But then, none of them had spent her youth sacrificing her higher education to keep her parents, who were neither sick nor disabled. My circumstances and life experience were quite different. Family duty, for us Armenians, was an unwritten moral code, "one for all and all for one". If I had left home to live alone, I would have ended up with a bad reputation and a guilty conscience.

Back to the real world. I started to learn touch typing. No more typing with only two fingers. I had to memorise the position of all the letters on the keyboard, and learn not only to touch type accurately but gradually to gain speed. It wasn't as easy as I thought. It needed a lot of practice. And as for Pitman's shorthand, it was like algebra to me, only instead of dealing with letters we were using squiggles, strokes, dots, dashes and signs, and I had to learn the correct position of those characters above, on or below the line. It was all phonetic and I had to study very hard to keep up with those youngsters who didn't have my difficulties. I struggled and I practised.

I also registered at an evening school for journalism. The course was not expensive and it was an ideal subject for me. I attended those sessions once a week where I met and made friends with Joyce, a charming and attractive English girl about my age. She was intelligent and very well read. We visited each other for tea and enjoyed the company. But unfortunately she moved to

London very soon after. Though I was sorry to lose her, somehow I felt I would see her again some day. I was right.

In the first two terms of my secretarial course, not only did I learn touch typing properly but also had the highest mark in shorthand theory. I needed another term for higher speed in both typing and shorthand. The headmistress was very happy with my results and was careful not to praise me in front of the others. I went to her office to thank her for her encouragement, and to tell her I was sorry I would not be able to continue the course. I did not give her my reasons, and she kept saying she could help me. Maybe she realised my problem was financial, who knows. I just said good-bye and left.

If I had stayed on, I wouldn't have been able to pay my weekly 30 shillings to the Hostel. My brother, the ever hopeful genius, found life in America difficult. He couldn't sell his inventions and wasn't allowed to stay or work, even depending on relations' hospitality was hard to accept. So, "la vie en rose" wasn't coming our way, at least not yet. It was obvious I had to take responsibility for myself. I gave notice at the college reluctantly. That would mean I could now pay the YWCA for a few more weeks. No hope from Diran, no job, no money. I was a worried woman once more.

CHAPTER 3   JOB-HUNTING

I survived until I paid my last 30 shillings to the warden and then I explained the situation to her. She was a kind Christian woman and she sympathised. I promised to pay as soon as I managed somehow. But how?

The news that I was destitute travelled soon enough to the girls. Some were kind and said they would look in papers to find me a job. Some others, not so. One girl said "Why don't you go home?". Good question. I didn't answer. I didn't even have the fare, besides, how could I inflict such a defeat on my parents who had high hopes on their children? Another one said "In your place I would have gone to Piccadilly". An easy way out maybe, but not for me. What upset me the most was when, I noticed sadly, some of them stopped leaving their purses lying carelessly about. That was the biggest blow. They probably thought I might be tempted.

It had now been six weeks that I hadn't paid the warden and she hadn't given me any signs that they would throw me out. In gratitude, I offered to help with the washing up for the whole house, 30 girls and staff, the kitchen sink full of dirty plates, pots and pans and cutlery, twice a day and three meals at weekends. Then I'd dry them and put everything away tidily where they belonged. I continued doing this for several weeks and I was thankful for still having a roof over my head and for not going hungry. Later on I learnt that the YWCA governors had been to a special board meeting with the warden about me, and since I was a practising Christian girl, they decided not to take any action. They believed in me and wanted to give me the opportunity to find my feet. I am very grateful to them for being so charitable.

I am Armenian, the race that prides itself for being the first Christian State in the world. Armenia is the country of my ancestors in the Caucasus, reduced to its present size through wars and atrocities. My Church is not only the defender of our religion but also the stronghold of Armenians scattered in the Diaspora. Through occupations and invasions the Church was like our Head of State. The Catholicos, the Supreme Patriarch of all Armenians, is like our Pope. I am not a historian nor a politician but I love my Church with all my heart, and the tiny little country called Armenia that I have never yet seen.

I was born in Istanbul. I was a Turkish subject once; I am a British citizen now and proud of it. I came to England in 1946 to follow my brother's plans and stayed on. In Manchester, where I went first, there was a large Armenian community, a beautiful church in Upper Brook Street. The Archbishop was friendly and invited me to sing in the choir. I also taught reading and writing in Armenian to the daughters of families who were kind to me: the Shahbenderians, Zeronians, Garabedians, Markarians and Middletons. A year later when I was in need, I should have asked them for help but I couldn't. Whether it was pride or shame or embarrassment, I don't know. I didn't want to be a charity case.

In the meantime my English friends at the hostel were scouring the appointments pages of the dailies for me. After a few unsuccessful enquiries there was just one which appealed to me as a possibility. It said: "Sec. wanted. Languages, good with figures". Could this be the one? No harm in trying. I wrote my first job application and instead of posting it, delivered it by hand so that it would be there first thing the next morning. This was a Thursday evening, and on the following Monday, early in the morning, there was a call for me from the Export Department of Dunlop Rubber Company, to attend for an interview. Panic. All the girls were very supportive. The names I remember now are: Jane, Jean, Janet, Joan, June, Julie, Joyce, Audrey, Anne, Bernice, Barbara, Dorothy, Marjory, Myfanwy, Pat, Yvonne. They may not be aware of it but they kept me going through my very traumatic days.

A reunion of visiting Manchester YWCA friends in the Sixties

Deprivation was not new to me, but in a foreign country where I was only allowed to stay as a student and not a permanent resident, and where I had to be financially independent and instead was reduced to nothing ... I was at a loss as to how to manage. God bless those wonderful YWCA Governors who allowed a foreign girl to remain without pressure in safe surroundings.

I always say that God has every time come to my rescue at the very last moment to make me appreciate His clemency. So, that Monday, with high hopes, I presented myself to the office of Mr.

Smith, the Export Sales Manager. He dismissed his secretary and ordered me to take a seat. He was early middle aged, a serious man with an unsmiling face, which was not very welcoming. I was not at all at ease. He asked about my qualifications. I told him how far I had got at college and that I had also worked back at home and had work experience in different capacities. "Figures?" "I am quite good at them." "Languages?" I said "Four." He asked me why I had come here. I told him I wanted to learn English and live here.

Short questions, short answers. After a few minutes of silent reflection, he ordered his secretary, Freda, to come back and dictated a telegram to the Home Office. He asked me to phone next Monday for the outcome. Without going much into details now, at a second attempt he eventually managed to get the Home Office's approval on condition that I was only allowed "TO WORK FOR DUNLOP RUBBER COMPANY'S EXPORT DEPT." He made me understand that he was engaging me on the strength of my knowledge of languages and that working with figures would be an advantage too.

I started working in a small office with three men and two other women. Apart from the secretarial work, I also kept their statistics books which recorded all the figures for exports and imports from all corners of the world where they had branches or associates, suppliers of raw rubber and importers of their products.

Those books were very large volumes in dimension and weight, all six of them, classified according to the geographical locations of their colonies and the Commonwealth countries and islands. For instance, if I didn't know where Leeward Islands were I couldn't find the right book. Mr. Smith was happy that my knowledge of geography wasn't bad either. Every month those huge volumes would be delivered to me and each one would cover my desk. I had to spend a whole day on the statistics. There were different columns of figures for import and export: raw rubber being imported and the various finished products going to their destinations.

At an age when computers were unheard of, I was doing mentally what a few key clicks would now do in one minute. At the end of the day, adding and subtracting from column to column horizontally, in tightly written small numbers, I would almost be cross-eyed. One day, Freda came in to reclaim the books. I said that I was sorry but there was a mistake somewhere I couldn't find and that I would continue checking. She said, "One mistake? That's nothing; no one has been able to do those books properly before."

I was a rotten typist, slow and not very accurate. I believe I was employed just for those books.

One day I was summoned to Mr. Smith's office. There were two gentlemen customers from Turkey who were here on business with us. Mr. Smith wanted me to translate the conversations and also to show them the sights. A car was waiting at the door to take us around the city. Mr. Smith introduced me to them with a certain pride: "This is Miss Sarafian. She can speak your language." When they were introduced to me I couldn't hide my surprise: they were Armenians from Istanbul. Naturally we were very pleased to have met. I took them to our Church first of all, where we were photographed with our Archbishop. Then off we went to Piccadilly and the shopping centre, and after a very interesting day we went back to the office where Mr. Smith welcomed two very satisfied customers and appreciated, I am sure, my assistance in securing a large order.

Every year the Dunlop Company held a talent competition for its staff in music, singing, dancing, juggling and acting. Auditions were taking place; I entered as a singer and was chosen as one of the finalists from the Manchester branch. We would all go to Birmingham where Dunlop contestants from all over the country would compete in the finals. My song was "J'attendrai" in French by Tino Rossi. When my turn came to go on stage in front of 600 - 700 people, I was petrified. My introduction as a French girl among all the English was applauded enthusiastically. I felt like a fraud, but what could I do at the last minute? Say "No, I am not French, I am Armenian?". What would I gain and who would care? I was being applauded before I had even made a sound, because being French was an attraction in itself. My performance was enhanced by the microphone and I got a rousing reception.

The BBC reporter who was interviewing all the contestants came to shake my hand saying "Mademoiselle, quel honneur" with a rather good accent to get a few words out of me. He wanted to know if I had come from Paris and asked other personal questions. I did not want to lie or make things up, I just wished it never happened. I thanked him and excused myself, bowed to the audience and left hurriedly. All the categories were judged, and I was one of the runners up in the singing. The winner who sang "One Fine Day", an aria from Puccini's Madame Butterfly, had a trained voice which wasn't fair on the rest of us and our team complained, as only amateurs were supposed to take part. But it was no use, she had strong support and a really magnificent voice. I have kept the programme of that concert to this day as a nostalgic memento.

Oh! Brother! I think Providence was using my brother to lead me to the next episode of my story. After many misadventures of his own, Diran was finally finding his feet, and in keeping with his promise, this time he definitely wanted me to go to America. For that, he explained to me, I had to get to London, because he himself had had trouble with the American Consul in Manchester, from whom he had obtained his visa two years ago, and he did not think the Consul would give me one.

Me going to London? He meant me to live there. I had just about managed to secure a job and accommodation in Manchester, and what a struggle that had been. I couldn't possibly abandon all this and start all over again. And where in London did he think I could stay with no job, no money? He was crazy. It was impossible. I had no one to rely on. But he was adamant: "You must". That was an order. "Dear God help me." Providence had to come to my rescue again...

Recently things had not been running smoothly in our little office of three women and three men. The youngest typist, everybody's teenage darling, would clock in every morning, type till lunch time, then disappear in the afternoon. So the rest of her letters would pile up on my desk. "She wasn't feeling very well" would be the reason given to me. Unfortunately, this state of affairs continued until I discovered that she was going off with her boyfriend every afternoon. I got really angry. I told the man who dictated the letters to me, "I am not going to do hers any more" and just dumped her pile back on her own desk.

Bob didn't think I could afford to be that assertive since he knew how badly I needed that job ... daringly he said "If you have any complaints go and see Mr. Smith!". That challenge was an invitation to reciprocate. I don't know what came over me. I got up, said "All right, I'll go then". I left my seat and walked down the corridor towards Mr. Smith's office. "Yea gods, what am I going to say?". I stood there for a few seconds trying to formulate what I "could" tell him. No, not about Bob and the girl typist. You didn't trouble Mr. Smith for silly office tittle-tattle. He was unapproachable, the most important person there.

I knocked. "Come in!" came his sharp voice. I entered as he was dictating to Freda. "Please, Mr. Smith, may I speak to you privately?" I said. He dismissed her and asked me to sit down. I started by telling a story that recently I was getting too many colds and the doctor advised me to move to the South. He was listening without looking at me. Maybe, he thought, I was going to hand in my notice. I continued after a pause. "Would it be possible to have a transfer to your London office, please?" He was speechless for a while and I was scared stiff in case he sacked me there and then.

"Do you know what you are asking me to do, Miss Sarafian? We will soon have two pregnant typists leaving, and now you. Is this really your reason?" I hung my head shamefacedly. "Yes." He picked up the phone and barked "Give me London!". Then he talked to someone he called John and said he was sending him one of the girls, "Do what you can" he said, then he listened to him and said, "Thanks". Turning to me he said "Go to the Travel Office now, they will give you a voucher to get a ticket to London tomorrow". I said "Tomorrow?". I was stunned. He said "Yes, you are lucky, as it happens they have a place and if you don't go now there is an applicant waiting for it on Monday". I didn't know how to thank him. He had a glint in his eye that meant 'I don't believe your story'. But he'd helped me just the same.

When I went back to our office a puzzled Bob said sarcastically, "Did you really go to Mr. Smith?". I said "Of course, and I've got an interview tomorrow in London". He couldn't believe his ears. He just stared, open-mouthed and dumbfounded.

CHAPTER 4 MOVE TO LONDON

The next day, at the London office of Dunlop in St. James's Street, I was given a typing test. I was trying to type a letter for the third time and still couldn't get it right. The new manager was very understanding. "You must be tired and nervous," he said, "you have a good reference from Manchester, this is just a formality. You can start in two weeks."

First and foremost, before leaving Manchester, I had to arrange for somewhere to stay in London. My warden gave me the address of a YWCA branch in London. I was lucky enough to find accommodation in a residential hostel not far from St. James's Street. It was in Onslow Gardens, in South Kensington. It was fantastic. I was getting a lot of help from On High, Providence was busy again. And my dear brother was being instrumental in shaping my future.

Diran and Dorothy

By this time, my brother had married an American girl from Columbia University; her name was Dorothy and she looked very nice in the photo that Diran sent me. One day she sent me the most fabulous gift anyone could wish for in those days of rationing: a big, heavy parcel full of chocolates, Hershey's and Cadbury's. It was absolutely unexpected. She wanted to give me a surprise - it was more than a surprise. What could I do with all that? I couldn't eat it all by myself, I couldn't hide it. Besides my room-mates were with me when I opened the box. We couldn't believe our eyes, we just kept looking. It was like a treasure trove. I felt guilty, and started offering them round, not realising that I would end up with nothing myself. As a result, though, I had a devoted following for a few days.

By now, I had managed to repay all my debts with the YWCA. I was also helped by the parcels of second-hand clothes my American cousins sent me. The clothes were almost new and very smart, they fitted me perfectly. Another time, I was sent a whole bag of nylon stockings with minor snags, which were quite unnoticeable. As I was very hard up at the time, I sold most of those nylons to the girls. They were so happy, as most of them walked about with bare legs because they didn't have enough coupons to buy stockings.

Before leaving, I thanked everyone for their kindness and support. I had contacted Joyce, who was already in London, asking her to meet me at St. Pancras Station on my arrival. She was sweetness itself. She gave me a hand in settling into my second floor room, which I was to share with two others. Joyce then walked me to Kensington Gardens. We sat by the Round Pond and watched the ducks. Walking back, she showed me the Royal Albert Hall and the Albert Memorial. I fell in love with Kensington.

Little did I know then that I would be living there for the rest of my life, until now 53 years later!

My new home wasn't quiet and secluded like the YWCA in Manchester. This was in a Royal Borough, with wide roads, fine architecture, the Park and not to forget the Armenian Church, all within walking distance. Joyce was living in a flat in Cromwell Road, which wasn't too far either. So, all I had to do was to familiarise myself with my new surroundings and get acquainted with my room-mates, and most of all, be in the good books of Miss Evans, the new Warden.

This Hostel was a large corner house on five floors, with no garden. The kitchen was in the basement, the office, dining room and lounge on the ground floor. The bedrooms were all upstairs on three floors.

Travelling to the office, I had to take the tube from South Kensington to Green Park and walk for five minutes. If Manchester was a culture shock for an Eastern girl like me, I can assure you London was yet another to my Mancunian self. The Metropolis would take anyone's breath away. There was so much to see, it was so crowded, noisy, there was traffic, hustle and bustle everywhere. Travelling by tube every morning and evening, in packed carriages, escalators whizzing up and down: all this was enough to make you dizzy. I just had to get used to commuting like all those hundreds of people. This was no life for the weak and the faint-hearted. We all had to earn a living, and life was expensive in the Capital.

My new office was large and had too many people working there for my liking. It was not an intimate circle of comrades as in Manchester. I couldn't stop myself from noticing how different everything was, compared to what I was used to. I couldn't change things, so I had to adapt, that's all there was to it.

There were sections in the office like unwalled compartments. Everyone knew his or her corner and desk, and also knew who was in charge of each section. I made friends with a quiet girl who was always alone at lunch time. It was easier to talk to people who were not boisterous. She was called Beatrice, and was from Chatham. I called her Bea. We used to walk through St. James's Park after the canteen lunch for about half an hour before going back to the office again. My job was just typing. I didn't really enjoy it very much, and I still wasn't proficient enough.

A few times, after lunch, I ventured down the road to Piccadilly. I was disappointed: the Piccadilly in Manchester was more spacious and had a garden in the square. Here, there was just a statue in the centre, on steps. I learnt that this was called Eros, and represented the God of Love. And all those shops, my goodness! I was afraid of losing track of time and being late for work. I was getting addicted to window shopping.

There was a porter at the street entrance and every time you went in or out you had to show your card. This was London, not the Dunlop in an industrial back-street of Manchester where nobody would take notice of you. This new culture shock was as intense as the first one. The office girls, like those at the Hostel, were all more sophisticated and fashion conscious. I started grooming myself, bought a women's magazine to give me ideas. I had to keep up with the rest of them.

I had seen a pair of shoes in a shop window, so beautiful and with a price tag beyond my means. I would go and look at them every day to see if they were still there. It was love at first sight! In the end, I spent a whole week's wages on the shoes and adored them. Many years later, when ankle straps were back in fashion, my daughter asked me if she could borrow them. They were still in good condition.

Now that my brother was married, his letters were not so frequent and I could breathe more freely. But he wouldn't give up on the American visa. When his letters were delayed I was less anxious, I didn't mind. There was plenty to occupy me. It was like a break. I enjoyed my freedom. I went to the cinema at the weekends. But I also had a polyphoto taken - that is, a series of photographs - as I was told that for an American visa, you needed front and profile shots.

*   *   *   *

I had been having some problems with my gums that I wanted to have checked, and after making enquiries, I found out there was an Armenian dentist not far from my Hostel. So, one Saturday morning I went to him without an appointment. The clinic in Wetherby Gardens, South Kensington, had a large waiting room with leather sofas. While I was looking through a magazine on the table, the door opened and there was the dentist in his white coat. He greeted me with "Good morning. Can I help you?" I immediately spoke to him in Armenian: "Do you speak Armenian?" He was astonished and grinned, "Of course, do come in." He asked my name and the other details he needed to complete my patient records. He checked my teeth and gums. It seemed there was nothing to worry about, I just had to use a mouthwash and not to brush very hard.

"I'll see you on Monday", he said when making me another appointment. I told him I was working and couldn't come before 6pm. He said that would be all right. I had just made my first dental appointment with Mr Gorgodian: little did I suspect that it would change the course of my life.

CHAPTER 5   A NEW ACQUAINTANCE

In our Church, the fête of the Virgin Mary's Assumption is celebrated in mid-August, the nearest Sunday to the 15th. It is a very holy day for us Armenians, we always go to church to celebrate, when we also have the ceremony of the blessing of grapes, a pagan custom, which through the ages was adopted by us as it was on the same day. People donate basketfuls of the fruit to put on the altar to be blessed during Mass. Afterwards, small bundles of grapes are distributed to the worshippers.

I was at St. Sarkis Church in Kensington that Assumption Sunday in August 1949, enjoying our beautiful service, when I realised there was someone standing right behind me breathing heavily, because of the heat, I guessed. I didn't want to turn round as that would be rude. But I was conscious of that person's presence.

When the service was over and I was able to look behind me, I was surprised to see my dentist whom I had only met the day before. We went out with the whole congregation where people started talking with each other. He saw me hurrying to leave, but caught up with me. He asked if I could go out to lunch with him, but I told him, "No thanks, my dinner is waiting for me at the hostel, I can't be late", smiled and left to walk away quickly.

At the Hostel, lunch was over, the others were having their puddings, but mine was being kept warm. I took it out of the oven and sat down to enjoy my roast dinner. I had just started my dessert when the telephone rang. Somebody answered and called out, "Miss Sarafian you're wanted on the phone". I thought it could be Joyce and picked up the receiver. But no, it was my dentist, asking me if I would like to go to Brighton with him that afternoon. I didn't know where that was, and he explained it was by the sea. I thought it would be late by the time we got there, but he reassured me that it was only one hour by train. "I can meet you at South Kensington Station in half an hour, all right?" I said "All right".

When the girls heard what had happened, they said, "Don't go if he hasn't got a car". "But", I said, "I promised!" Anyway, I met him as arranged. The train from Victoria took almost an hour. It was a fine day; we sat on the Pier and had tea.

Perhaps it was odd that I accepted an invitation from a man knowing so little about him. He was almost a stranger to me, as I was to him. But we were both mature people. He was serious and dignified. After all, he was a professional man, and this was just a simple outing. Nothing to read into it. Obviously, he was enjoying my company, though the conversation was practically one-sided as I was doing most of the talking. We started off by talking about the day's church service, religion, life and death. And, was there life after death? As I had briefly done a correspondence course years before about the occult (through the Arcane School in the USA whose president was Alice Bailey), I was convinced about its existence. I had learnt about reincarnation, the astral body, the laws of Karma, gurus and suchlike. Bits of information that escape me now, but the conviction stays.

For the first time in the three years I had been in England, I was having a conversation which had nothing to do with office, hostel, cost of living, my brother, America and my dead-end life. Physically, my companion was no Gregory Peck - the actor was then my heart-throb, tall, dark and handsome. My companion had dark hair all right, though slightly greying at the temples, and was about my height – but handsome? I couldn't say, as I wasn't that interested at this stage, it wasn't an issue. He was wearing glasses and looked kind and insecure or shy - a little gauche and uneasy.

Brighton Promenade, the day after we first met

After a simple tea and cakes, we got up for a stroll and right on the promenade, a street photographer took a quick snapshot of us together. For a pound, he promised to send a copy to my address. I was wearing a smart red dress sent to me from America, had a large straw hat I had bought in Paris, when I visited by aunt and uncle in the spring, and was wearing my new beautiful shoes. I had had no time to change after the church service and only grabbed the hat to protect me from the sun at the seaside. He was dressed in casual clothes, and gave the impression that he either didn't care about his appearance, or didn't know how to. I guessed there was no woman in his life.

At that time, I didn't even know his Christian name, so I didn't call him anything. He knew mine as he had it on his records. No personal questions were asked; it was all very formal. He called me, "Oriort" which means "Miss" in Armenian. He was neither a Romeo nor a flatterer, he was just a polite gentleman.

He knew I had to be back at 10pm, so we took the next train to Victoria and a taxi from there to return me to the Hostel on time. There was no need to fix a further date as I had an appointment with him the next day at 6pm. My impression? A brief encounter with a lonely man. Even though it was a casual acquaintance, he was my dentist and a gentleman, and that was that. I was going to go to America anyway, there was no point in forming meaningful friendships.

I didn't want to think about him, but somehow, he was there, still fresh in my memory. He impressed me as being kind, shy, serious and alone. Was he alone? Did he have a wife? Anyway, that wasn't my business. I was soon going to America, and goodbye everybody!

If I was going to go to America, shouldn't I begin organising my trip? But where to start? I made tentative enquiries with travel agents and shipping companies. The costs of flying or going by sea were equally expensive, and I had no money. I was just about earning my keep. My dear brother hadn't mentioned sending my fare. It was all very well to say, "Go to London" or "You must come to America", but how?

I had always worshipped my brother, I had put him on a pedestal as my hero, a kind of looking up to him that also inspired fear. From my childhood days, I remember, I had to obey, or else! I remember, when playing in the street, he would punish me by making me stand on one foot, and when I was tired, all he would say was "change legs" and I can't remember now what my crime was in the first place. Or else! What? For Heaven's sake, I was 29 now, it was ridiculous to depend on him or be scared of him. That's why I came to London, because he ordered me to, and it wasn't easy. But going to America? Even if it were made possible, would I like it there? And what about his new wife? Would she want me around? It would be even further away from my parents, those poor creatures still waiting in suspense, waiting for the time when their son would ask them to go and live with him. Now that he was married to an American girl, that seemed less and less likely.

The next day after work, I just about managed to arrive on time for my dental appointment. At Green Park, the platform was very crowded and I missed a train. I explained this to him when I was sitting in his chair, in the surgery, that very nearly I didn't make it and I didn't think I could have any further appointments in the evening. He said, "You were the last one anyway, it wouldn't matter, I would have waited."

When the treatment was over - it was just a small filling - he said, "Your teeth are perfect, I don't think you need anything done for the time being. But I'd like to see you again, if I may?" I got up, I didn't know what to say. He broke the silence, "I'm going to have a short break and am going to Paris for a week. Could I call you on my return?" How to reply?

He was a nice man, there was no harm in having a casual friend, after all, until I left England. But I didn't want to give him false hopes, so I told him about my brother and my plans to go to America. I said that I wouldn't be staying in London very long, but if he wanted to meet again, then I didn't mind. He said, "America? When are you going?" and when I replied that I would be applying for a visa soon, he went very quiet. I picked up my handbag, ready to leave. I wished him a good holiday. He shook my hand warmly, but rather briefly. I walked away to the Hostel where my dinner was being kept warm yet again. I couldn't forget the look on his face when leaving. He looked disappointed.

A few days later, I received a postcard from him, that I still keep in my drawer. "Dear Miss Sarafian, Paris is beautiful and the weather is nice too. See you when I come back. Regards" and signature, Krikor Gorgodian.

He did call me on his return and we fixed a date for one evening to go out to dinner together. I think it was a restaurant in South Kensington. He met me at the station after work and we walked, it wasn't too far. When we sat down, he said "I've got something for you. I hope you like it."

It was a small packet gift-wrapped. He said "Open it, please". I was embarrassed. It was perfume, Chanel No. 5 in a white and gold box. It was the very first perfume that anybody had given me and I knew it to be very expensive. I thanked him and he smiled, and it was the first time that I had seen him smile. Then he said, "I've got another little something for you, I hope you'll like it too." In a long narrow box there was an ivory necklace, very attractive.

I said, "But why? It isn't my birthday or anything, it's too much!" He then said, "When you go to America, you may remember me by it ..."

I don't know whether it was the wine or the rich food, or the whole evening with all the happenings. I wasn't used to eating out, getting presents and having an admirer. I was overwhelmed. He talked to me about Paris, the interesting places he had been. He said that he would have enjoyed it even better had he had a good travelling companion. For once I was tongue-tied and he did most of the talking between mouthfuls. Afterwards, I didn't want to go to his flat for coffee. I told him I had to get up early for work. So he walked me back to my Hostel.

The next morning, I woke up with a terrible migraine. So I phoned the office to apologise and said I would go in the afternoon. I felt better a bit later, and presented myself at the office apologising once again. One of the "Head" Ladies said, "You had a visitor, unfortunately you missed him".

"Visitor?" I asked. She said "Yes" and in the full hearing of everyone around, she said, "Mr. Smith, the Export Sales Manager from Manchester. He was here for a board meeting. He asked after you and said, please give my regards to Miss Sarafian, tell her that I cannot replace her."

I think I went bright red. That was the nicest praise anyone could give me. I was sorry to have missed him, such a kind man, who could have refused to help me when it was a most inconvenient time for him too, instead of which he went out of his way to give me assistance and excellent references. Behind that unsmiling morose face, there was a man with a golden heart.

I sat at my desk trying to concentrate on my work. I felt everyone's eyes on me. Please God, don't let me make mistakes again! After all that praise, they may wonder what exceptional qualities I had that someone like Mr. Smith would bother to look for me and also say that he could not "replace" me. As far as they were concerned, there was nothing outstanding in my performance as a secretary.

I felt uneasy and talked to Bea about this, and also told her about the special work I did for Mr. Smith. I had a feeling she spread that information with discretion. There were no more side glances in my direction. And anyway, as this was not just the Export Department, they had no use for my other talents! Just as well, at the moment, I couldn't cope with anything so stressful.

As it was, my mind was not on my work, it was quite preoccupied with new problems I did not know how to solve. Was I going to America? The way things were going, I was not even taking any steps or trying to do anything about it. I should be going to the American Consulate to find out about the process, fill in forms or applications, get a visa, secure a passage or a flight with a travel agent, and last but not least, find the money. Wasn't it ridiculous to suggest that I could do all that by sitting on my backside? Or, did I expect a miracle to happen and a ticket to materialise out of thin air?

It had also just occurred to me that my dentist friend might think I was making all this up. But why should I do such a thing? He called me again that evening and we went for a walk towards the Park. I was very quiet and he wondered if he had offended me the night before. I said, "no, nothing to do with you" and burst into tears.

We sat on a bench. He insisted, "What is the matter?" He was concerned. At that time, the garden wasn't crowded. "Please tell me, what happened?" My words came out in a torrent, I just told him the truth, in short sentences, that my brother was pressing me to join him in America but I couldn't go through with it, I couldn't even buy my ticket.

He kept quiet for a while, and then asked "Do you really want to go very badly? Must you?"

"I don't know. Until now, I've done everything my brother has told me to do, but now he is married things have changed and I am so confused." He had no doubt about my sincerity, I wasn't putting on an act.

He put his hand on mine and squeezed gently. "Don't worry, you go and get your visa and I'll lend you the money to buy your ticket."

I pulled my hand away, "No."

Gently, he persisted, "I am only going to lend it to you, you can pay it back when you can, all right?"

I looked away, I couldn't even thank him. Why was he being so generous? I couldn't understand why he made that offer. Did he really want me to go? I kept quiet. It was getting dark. Finally, we got up, we hardly said anything. When leaving me at my door, he just said, "Don't worry. And think about it".

I did think about it. I did nothing but think about it. I couldn't make out his true feelings, or even my own feelings about all these conflicting situations. One minute I was telling myself there was no harm in being just good friends with him until I left, the next minute, I was not sure what to make of this turn of events. I was afraid all this would affect my work at the office. I tried to put these thoughts behind me. When he phoned me the next day, I just told him I needed some space and not to call me for a few days.

That weekend, I didn't go out. I took a long, hard look at things. I tried to put my options in perspective. Did I have a choice one way or another? Until now, all my thoughts, all my actions were governed by my brother, Diran, as if no one else mattered. But what about him? Had I become too much of an obligation or burden for him? He did have a right to his own life, to his wife and future family. And if I went to America, would he still be in charge of me and would I have to start adapting all over again? I had done nothing but adapt these last few years. I had had enough.

CHAPTER 6   MY BROTHER DIRAN

My childhood was spent in a loving family. My father wasn't very demonstrative, but my mother was all emotions. My brother was six and a half years older than me. As a boy, he was very naughty and a tearaway. Played in the streets all day during the holidays, and led a gang of boys against another gang. My mother was always apologising to other mothers for my brother's actions.

I never forget, one day she dressed me in a new dress she had made (she made all my clothes and her own), and warned me not to tell Diran that we were going to the "Jardin", which was an exclusive little park in Taksim square with an entrance fee. In those days, I suppose, my father must have been employed, so we had the money to go.

Age six, in a new dress my mother made for me

When we met the gang in the street, my brother shouted, "where are you off to?" My mother replied, "Nowhere special, just window-shopping". He didn't believe her, bent down to my level and asked, "Where are you going, sweetie?" Then me, little innocent lamb, said "Diran, we are not going to the Jardin". I was being obedient to my mother and yet with such an obvious lie, my clever brother understood immediately. "That's it, you are going to the Jardin", and called his gang over. They climbed over fences and walls and played havoc until an usher chased them out. My poor mother, embarrassed, tried to keep her composure and pretend she didn't know him.

My brother and I, playing in the street

Diran had too much energy he couldn't use otherwise. He was very bright at school, he excelled in Maths without even trying. At the age of 14, he wished to go to Venice, the continuation of the intermediate school he had attended in Istanbul. Most of his classmates would be going too, the Mourat Raphaelian boarding college run by friars. He went for a scholarship, and managed to pass all his exams to receive a grant for the duration of his schooling. We didn't see him until he graduated, because we couldn't afford the return fares.

On the eve of Diran's departure for Venice

When my brother returned he was nearly 19, a tall young man, completely changed under the strict discipline of the Mechitarist Brothers. Diran didn't stay long with us; he was raring to go to university in Paris, where my mother's sister and brother lived. They had only a small flat, but made room for their nephew. He immediately enrolled at the Sorbonne. Despite the fact that his main language was Italian and he did not arrive until the end of the term, Diran passed the Maths exams with flying colours and had the highest marks.

My aunt and uncle, Mo and Daida (as we children called them) were just about making a living. Mo was doing "haute couture" for a firm and Daida worked at Renaults car factory. My brother ended up living with them for 14 years from 1932 onwards. After he had gained his Maths degree, he went to Toulouse, to the famous Polytechnic, to gain a degree in Electro-mechanical Engineering.

Now, he had a second feather in his cap, but still no work. The war was making lives very difficult for everyone, everywhere. My brother hadn't had it at all easy, either. Money was short, causing deprivation for him in Paris and us back in Istanbul. My father would have preferred him to go into teaching instead, to earn a salary, but my mother, always ambitious for her extremely bright son, wanted the best for him. His future was of utmost importance in all our thoughts, and he was worth every sacrifice. We never grumbled or grudged our efforts. He was the apple of our eyes. Diran the genius - and (we hoped) our saviour. We were all trusting that the tree we so lovingly tended would soon bear fruit.

What an ominous task for him! Indeed, without his initiative, I would still be living in Istanbul, doing thankless jobs. Marriage was out of question. I had baggage: my parents. I had had a couple of boyfriends, a couple of suitors, and was even engaged briefly against my parents' wishes though this did not work out (just as well). He was tall, dark and handsome, but nothing more. The minute my brother decided things had to change, he took charge and started with me.

In the meantime, Diran was hoping to be able to sell another discovery very soon, a very important invention indeed: The Noiseless Railway. He had discovered a method by which the train rails would not have the usual gaps at the end, which caused all the noise, but would overlap to allow for expansion or shrinkage during weather changes. This method would eliminate the shake and tick-tack noise when the wheels dropped in the gaps between the tracks. He arranged meetings with the heads of both Railways and Underground executives in England. He was told that steel was in short supply at the time, and they could not afford to change the whole country's network structure. In America, they were not interested either. Trains were not a priority for domestic travel. Some other projects also ended in nothing.

Because he could not afford to pay the yearly subscription fees at the Patent Office, his inventions became state or public property. He had intelligence, courage, but no luck or business acumen. In many ways, he still expected the world to be running on good values. He spent five years cloistered behind school walls, at a college run by monks, unaware of everyday conditions in life. He was a scientist, a pure mathematician, and had to learn the hard way to be streetwise. Now that he was married, he had to build a home and have a family.

And where would I come in? Enough is enough! I should not expect anything from him anymore. Maybe I should not go to

America after all. And, what then? Stay here? I was having serious doubts about the state of my affairs. Going to America was becoming a joke. I was confused, undecided and bewildered. Three years previously, I came from Istanbul to learn English and follow my brother to America. Now things had changed so much. I didn't want to be a burden to him any longer. I ought to be independent. I had got a job, I had somewhere to live: what about the future, and what was going to happen to my parents? They were still hoping for big things from their children. In Turkey, there were no such things as pensions or welfare benefits - not for us minorities anyway. If you didn't have a job or savings, you were finished, unless your family helped you. Now was the time for Providence to come to my rescue again.

CHAPTER 7   A SERIOUS PROPOSAL

At the weekend, Saturday afternoon, Krikor called and said, "I have just finished surgery, shall we go somewhere to eat?"

I was not prepared for this, I didn't want to spend a whole afternoon with him. "I am busy right now, maybe another time."

"I'll let you finish what you are doing, I'd like to take you to the Open Air Theatre in Regent's Park tonight. If you promise to come, I'll get tickets right now."

I did not know there was an Open Air Theatre. "What are they showing?" "The Taming of the Shrew." I did not want to show my ignorance of Shakespeare either, and ask what it was about. He insisted, "It'll do you good, Shakespeare will change your mood". So we went.

I was surprised to see a full house, and such an appreciative audience too. I read the summary in the programme. To my surprise, I enjoyed the play even though the language of that period was beyond me. Krikor was tactful enough not to ask if I could follow the plot. The open air and the play managed to dispel my darker mood. We walked to the Underground. At South Kensington Station, he asked me to his flat for coffee. I declined, "No coffee at night". He then suggested, "I've got a lovely liqueur from Paris, you will love it, it's very light. Please come."

His surgery and flat were leased from the previous dentist's widow, who owned the whole five-storey house. He had rooms on three floors: bedroom on the first floor with a shared bathroom, surgery and waiting room on the ground floor, and his workshop in the basement. His waiting room was spacious, with a leather three piece suite and antique furniture, and this also served as his private sitting room.

The Bénédictine, as he called it, was delicious indeed. I only had a little bit but already felt its effect. I was not used to alcohol, though it was light and sweet. "Some more?" "No thanks, I must go, it is late."

Krikor asked if I would be going to Church the next day, and if he could take me to lunch afterwards. How could he be so persistent when he knew I could not sustain a long friendship? Didn't he believe I was going to America?

I said, "I've got a lot of problems to sort out. I'm not sure what I'm going to do yet. I can't keep going out, I need time to consider everything and reach a decision."

"Does that mean that you may not be going?" he asked.

I raised my voice, "I don't know, don't ask me any questions, I don't know the answers". Again the floodgates opened, and I started crying. I was ashamed of my weakness, just letting it go like a cry-baby.

He said, "The offer stands, you know, if that's what is worrying you".

"I am not sure what is best, there are so many things to consider, I have no one to give me advice, no one!"

He came and sat down beside me. "I am here, I am your friend." Pause. "Do you really have to go? Please don't go, stay here" and lifted my face in his hands. I could not look in his eyes.

"Stay, please."

"Why, where?"

"Stay here, with me, I need you."

What did he mean by that? I wiped my eyes and blew my nose. "Do you need a typist?" Was I thick or something, or I was pretending to be, or maybe, I wanted him to spell it out.

"Don't you understand, I think I need you always to be with me, there is no need for you to go to America. Your brother is married now, it is your turn to find a life partner. What do you say?"

I was spellbound, I could not take it in. So it was true, he meant it. "I shall have to ask my brother".

"Did he ask you when he got married?"

"But he doesn't know you, and I haven't said anything."

He was holding my hand, "Shall I write to him for his approval, or do you want me to write to your parents?"

Things were going too fast for my liking, it was like a "fait-accompli". I said, "I must think. I'll see you tomorrow at Church, I must go now".

He said, "I'll walk you to your door". When he was leaving, he just bent down and kissed my hand.

*   *   *   *

What a night that was! How could I promise anything when I myself didn't know him, or much about him. Who was he? How old was he? What if he was already married? Perhaps he had a couple of kids somewhere. Was I that desperate to even consider a serious liaison, marriage, just like that? I couldn't say anything to my parents or to my brother because I didn't know Krikor well enough. All right, I knew he was kind, decent, professional. But that was about all. As far as looks were concerned, he was mildly attractive, if you looked in his eyes long enough. Later some people said they thought he looked like Clark Gable because he had a small moustache like his. There was something sad about his expression that gave him an air of seriousness. He was much older than me, maybe late thirties, I couldn't tell. I liked him a lot and trusted him, but was that enough? Things we had in common were that we were both Armenian, both alone and lonely; we seemed to be thrown together in a foreign country, yet again by Providence.

I went to bed with all those thoughts twirling in my head and woke up with them still there. After breakfast, I got dressed to go to Church, my mind still working non-stop. His words had stopped short of saying, "Would you marry me?" and that was bothering me a lot. He had not said that. I didn't know what he meant by "partner". As far as I knew that term was used in business only.

During the Service I prayed a lot for guidance. I think he must have arrived later because he was standing at the back. We went out together. "I hope you haven't asked for your dinner to be kept warm for you". "No I haven't". "How do you feel now?" "I am not sure. Can't decide."

We sat down to lunch at our familiar place in a secluded corner of the restaurant. "Let's eat first." We chose a simple Sunday roast.

Afterwards we automatically walked towards the Park. Kensington Gardens was becoming our thinking ground. It was still warm, though autumn was showing its signs with a covering of rust everywhere.

An empty bench was waiting for us. "Now, do you want to ask me any questions?" He knew what I was thinking.

"Yes, I think so. I don't really know much about you, and you don't know anything about me either."

"I know enough about you, that is sufficient for now. I know you have your famous brother, your parents, and also know that this question of going to America is causing you a lot of worry."

"I've got a job at the moment and somewhere to stay."

He said "Can't you see? You can't stay forever in a room with two others. You have done this kind of thing for three years now; that cannot be a permanent situation. It is time you had your own privacy and your own life. You cannot be sure that going to America is going to solve your problems. It all depends on your brother and his plans for you. What if you regret it? Isn't it time for you to have your own home, and be independent?"

He had said everything that was already in my thoughts, and I kept silent. I just couldn't find anything to say. I was looking away from him, into the distance, the birds, the trees.

He was now holding my hands. I knew what he was going to say next and I wasn't sure of my response. I avoided answering. I started instead "Tell me about yourself. You know who I am and about my family. I don't know anything about yours."

He said, "All right, I have just got an old aunt in Beirut; no one else."

"No family? You're not married?"

"No. I am a bachelor. I left the army only two years ago, I haven't been here long and I don't know many people. I'm nearly forty; my parents, sister and brother perished during the atrocities of 1915. I was rescued and later brought up in an orphanage".

It had all come out in one breath. With a small sigh he turned away.

How sad all this was. I didn't want to question him further. Later I would learn more about his schooling, his graduating from the American University of Beirut and going to the East to join the British Army in Rangoon as the dental surgeon of their regiment, from which he was discharged in 1947 and came to London.

"Don't you have any friends here?"

"Yes, a couple from the army."

"Any Armenians?"

"Not many. I have a doctor friend from University, and a few patients invited me over, also I met more people at community functions."

It was so peaceful in that part of the Park. Couples were strolling arm in arm. Young parents were pushing prams, toddlers were skipping about joyfully. Couples, families, children. Was this what life was about? Taking stock of mine I realised my biological clock was ticking fast, I was 29. Some people would call me an old maid. What was I expecting from life? Maybe at last I had arrived where I was supposed to. The turning point.

We were both watching all the passers-by. We didn't talk. Silence can say so much at times. We were looking at angelic little children frolicking about right in front of us. The sight was so attractive, it was like a picture. Their laughter was filling the air, giggle upon giggle. Such a contrast with our seriousness. You couldn't help but smile, and feel happy for them. What a joy they must be for their parents, I thought.

Suddenly he squeezed my hand and whispered softly in my ear. "Will you give me a little girl like that?" My heart was going to burst; at last he had just said what he wanted to say all along. Was this what I was waiting for, was it meant to be a proposal? But it wasn't a proper question, and I wasn't sure of my answer. He wasn't a talkative man and it was difficult for him to say what had been troubling him so badly. He has never been as eloquent as he was that day. He must have summoned all his courage to talk openly of his deep desire, his longing of ultimate fulfilment with a family and a loving wife, a soul-mate.

In response I just put my head on his shoulder. It was very comforting.

Providence had done its job again ... It gave us the opportunity to seize what it offered with both hands and not let it slip. No doubt there was mutual sympathy. He made it obvious he liked me, or even loved me to commit himself in all seriousness, and he had dispelled all my doubts; I was very fond of him too. Surely all this was the first step towards love. We had the maturity to understand the implications of this agreement which wasn't taken lightly; we were both sensible enough to recognise our inner feelings and hope we would be compatible, learn to give and take.

A big weight was lifted from my shoulders, and he was smiling again. The agony was over. There would be no more discussions about America. I was here to stay.

When we got up after a long while, he just said "Will you write to your brother?"

"Yes, I am not going to go."

CHAPTER 8   MERGING BACKGROUNDS

I did write to my brother and to my parents. They were not at all pleased. Diran objected that now I would not be able to go to America and he wouldn't be able to help any more; a ridiculous suggestion that I might be infatuated by "that man" who had seduced me and I was spoiling family plans.

This wasn't a game and I didn't want to be the pawn in the middle. I had had enough. I felt very assertive and replied immediately that I was already engaged and there was nothing more to say on the matter.

I wasn't engaged yet of course, that would come later. I just wanted to put an end to their opposition. I had made my choice and had no more doubts. I was confident and resolute. I knew Providence threw us together and our union was meant to be.

Krikor was longing to have his own nest, to start a family, protect and provide, give and receive affection, with the right person, and that was me! And on reflection, I thought he was the right person for me too. I understood later on that it was not just a little girl he wanted. He had never had a family of his own. After losing his parents as a young child in 1915 in Sivas, he was miraculously saved by a Kurdish couple who cared for him for a few years in utterly primitive conditions. He told me later on that they were so poor that he had no shoes on his feet. He was given a goat to take to the fields to graze.

The village children knew he wasn't one of them, and they used to chase him and throw stones at him shouting "Gâvurun oğlu", which means "Son of infidel". That way he never forgot his own origin and his Armenian identity.

When the Armenian Committee searching for Armenian orphans eventually traced him, he voluntarily went with them despite the cries of his adoptive mother, who had genuinely loved and cared for him.

He grew up in an orphanage without parental love and warmth. He later found his father's sister who gave him shelter and a home for a few years. He was a late starter, but through sheer hard work managed to work his way up and be admitted at the American University of Beirut, where he graduated later as a Dental Surgeon.

Not being an extrovert as a young man, he made few friends. When he started practising and earned enough money, he had a house built for his old auntie, with extra rooms for letting out to bring her an income. Thus, having done his duty, he went to India first replacing an Armenian dentist at his surgery for a year, then moving to Burma where he signed up in the British army in Rangoon as the regiment's dental surgeon. Discharged at the end of the war, he chose to go to England. He sailed out of Rangoon on March 1st with two others, via Ceylon, Suez, Malta and reached Southampton on 31st March 1947.

Once in London, he had to take a special course on dentistry at Guys Hospital for six months to obtain the British equivalent of his degree. He leased a surgery and living accommodation for five years at Wetherby Gardens in London SW7 where I met him two years later in 1949. As our friendship developed and we agreed to join our destinies, we were both mature and level headed. There was no infatuation, we were not blindly in love (at least not on my part), nor calculating. We had given the situation a lot of thought and went ahead seriously and confidently. We were ideal candidates for the scenario that he probably had in mind right from the beginning, and while the opportunity made itself available it would have been foolish to ignore it, lest it all vanished with the wind. This was probably the most daring decision of his life and he took it with both hands.

He didn't ask too many questions, he wasn't concerned as to whether I could cook or was a good housekeeper. He wasn't domesticated nor was I. He used to eat out and his flat was cleaned by the housekeeper. His washing went to the laundry service. He had never been close enough to anyone to spend evenings together in a cosy atmosphere.

On the other hand, I myself was neither a homemaker nor good in the kitchen. All my life, from my school days until I left Istanbul, my mother had done everything for me. I had never done anything to help her around the flat. I was like the man of the house, the breadwinner, tired after a day's work. I didn't like housework anyway, and to be truthful, I still don't. And when I found myself in the deep end, I didn't know where to start and how to keep an orderly home.

Struggling with all the modern conveniences at my disposal, I wondered how my mother ever managed in her makeshift kitchen in Istanbul, without running hot water, without gas and a proper cooker, no fridge, no washing machine, in a confined uncomfortable flat, which was ice cold in the winter and boiling hot in the summer, under a tin roof that was hell. I bless my long-suffering mother every day and regret I wasn't more understanding and patient with her.

My mother came from a well known and wealthy family. Her father, a self-made successful businessman in his hometown of Adapazar (a town in Turkey), lost all his fortune during the 1915 exodus - his possessions, his home, his business, his properties. The whole family was deported to the depths of Anatolia. It was a miracle they survived and at the end they managed to go to Istanbul to start a new life from scratch, by selling their jewellery and the few remaining gold sovereigns that my grandfather had been hiding in his body-belt. My mother was pregnant with me.

I was born on 28th July 1920. Once my mother had had servants; now she had to make do with primitive commodities. You get used to making sacrifices, putting up with bare necessities. You are conditioned to these basics and just exist from day to day. From my schooldays onwards our family's living standards went down and down, so much so that my father was unable to pay my school fees. Eventually they were scrapped altogether. It was an "Azkayin Varjaran" (Armenian National School), and I was one of the few who were admitted free. In those days I didn't realise how humiliating this was. I was in my final year and it was at that time that my brother decided I should be going to a French school to improve my knowledge of that language. He sent me the fees from Paris and I was enrolled at the nearest school to my home. He was making plans for me already, while all I had to do was pass my exams year after year.

When my school years were over and university was out of my reach for financial reasons, I started looking for a job. I didn't know what I could do as I wasn't trained for anything. The knowledge you amass through history and science books doesn't necessarily prepare you for office work. I found a job eventually. The boss, a tyrant, an Armenian nouveau riche and control freak, used to shower us with insults like a market trader to get things done, shouting and swearing and calling us names. I stuck with that place for over four years through necessity until I couldn't take it anymore.

It was time to move on, but I didn't leave until I secured myself another job. Luckily I was accepted by another Armenian firm, The Horasandjians Stationery Establishment. There was an atmosphere of quiet aristocracy. The owners were very civilised, educated and admirable people, who were strict but kind and fair. What a contrast! I stayed there until it was finally decided that I was going to England. I remember my boss Aram, the senior partner, getting up to wish me good luck and shaking my hand warmly. I was sorry to leave them. Years later, I heard they had moved to Buenos Aires.

*   *   *   *

Until now, I've been writing about things from the past. It's been hard, not only because I couldn't remember everything that easily, but also because I didn't want to write everything, even though I was getting deeper and deeper into details. Now I have come so far, I would like to bring my story to an end without disrupting the balance after such a lengthy beginning. I couldn't possibly say "he proposed and I accepted, we got married and had not one but three daughters and everything was perfect".

No. It wasn't that simple. I couldn't fast-forward 30 years of married life in one paragraph. I had worked hard to remember things from the past, not from yesterday but from half a century ago. And I must admit my memory isn't very sharp anymore. Not only was it time consuming but it was also mentally exhausting. I had to relive all my past in full colour, in every detail if possible. I went down memory lane, I checked my diaries, my old articles in the newspaper and was amazed as to how much I had forgotten. Some things you never forget, they are readily available, especially in old age, when you live in the past anyway.

During the search, feelings come alive, even passions that cannot be consumed anymore. You remember the sound of a voice, a certain chesty cough, or a grunt, or a snore; you can still hear them if you close your eyes and force yourself to believe they are real and that you are not imagining. You even sometimes think you can smell certain familiar scents, you bury yourself deeper and deeper into long gone days to seize the moment and hold on to it. Contemplation of senses so fugitive or maybe spiritual. You chase fleeting moments of contentment you don't want to let go, you hang on to your inner turmoils. It is painful and immensely profound, almost occult, out of this world. You want to be part of it. The harder you try the faster it escapes you. Immeasurable elations that cannot be translated into words. They are private, very private indeed; the unspeakable closeness of shared moments, like a dream that is interrupted on awakening and cannot be recaptured however hard you try. Then you've lost it. It was but an illusion. I believe that in such moments I may have visited my astral body, in spiritual elevations, that can only occur in the sub-conscious.

On a practical level I am not an authority on anything. My life is full of mistakes, like a patchwork of dark and light colours, with some pretty patterns and some ugly ones. I sometimes feel embarrassed for a few lapses that I put down to ignorance or lack of parental guidance. My parents were simple people with old values and puritanical convictions, who could not imagine that their children could do unacceptable things like kissing somebody, for instance. My mother would have been horrified if she knew I had been kissed. And we all know that in those days a kiss was just a gentle kiss, just touching of the lips, not the mouth devouring type of present times. It would be the beginning of a romance not an affair.

I was a romantic girl. I would read all the books from the library of my French school, clean and moral love stories that make an adolescent girl dream of a gallant suitor, fall in love and get married and be blissfully happy ever after. If only I could meet such a man who would also take me "lock stock and barrel" and my parents too.

In my dream world, I would go on trying remember some things which were seemingly trivial but important enough to stir my inner self, usually ending up crying and not be able to continue further. Disappointed, I tried to harden myself by being objective, as if I was writing simple fiction, recording events that followed on from each other without leaving their mark on me. I was kidding myself. Some details were so unreal, like part of a dream that on waking vanishes, like shadows that are behind you and cannot be caught.

I relived some incidents in my memories many times over, so much so that sometimes I felt uncomfortable. There was a sense that I might be disturbing my beloved husband's spirit. I remember from my past occult lessons that you should leave spirits well alone. You don't bring them down to your level. They should detach themselves from us. They have a gradual transportation into higher spheres. Because, otherwise, they will suffer with us and for us, at not being of any practical assistance. We should not trouble them. They will never come down to our level, just the opposite, if anything, we will one day join them on a higher astral level.

I also learnt that all the people you have been involved with in this life have also been part of your past life. Gender is irrelevant. The soul, the spirit is the same under a different guise. My husband could have been my son or father, or even my sister in my previous life. The feelings of sympathy or antipathy would continue through. I was given a simple example to understand those theories. "A new life is like picking up the knitting you left unfinished the night before, until you put it down again when your life is over this time, ready for the next." I believe the knitting will not be over until we have exhausted all our incarnations, each time paying for past sins we left unredeemed..

That is why we suffer sometimes so unnecessarily; we wonder what we have done to deserve this. That is due to the Law Of Karma. You reap what you have sown.

Many saints gave up the life of enjoyment, of riches and pleasure, to reach the state of purity, sanctity and the final godliness. Which is our aim eventually, to become one with God. And Jesus himself was the last reincarnation of several past lives until he became Christ, the Son of God, and gave up his human existence for elevation to godliness.

I am sure this is not convincing enough for most people. I do not claim to be an authority on occult, only a learner, or rather a past learner. Unfortunately my education on this subject was on an elementary level and was interrupted by more pressing terrestrial matters. I just couldn't find either the time or the peaceful state of mind for meditation.

CHAPTER 9 FINALLY ENGAGED

I had come to admire the man I was going to marry. The days were going fast, like the reel of a film. We were still trying to understand each other, and get used to each other's ways. Until now, in my life, I had learnt to adapt myself to most hazards, and I was more than ready to try again. This time it was going to be for good. It would be give and take come what may.

He hated small talk, he wasn't good at it. He couldn't express his feelings in words easily. He didn't say to me "Darling I love you, will you marry me?" He was almost tongue tied, but he knew that if he didn't act quickly enough he would lose me. Later on, after getting married, he wasn't in the habit of giving me red roses for my birthday, or champagne, or making any kind of demonstration of love, or extravagant gestures. Most women liked to be flattered and pampered - I didn't need to be.

We had no false pretences in our lives. I still wonder though, how he managed to bring me presents from Paris when he had only known me for 48 hours! That was the pluckiest thing he had done in his life. He must have been driven by a very strong motive. Could that be love at first sight? If so, he probably had to suppress his feelings, maybe due to insecurity or self consciousness, or fear of rejection. In which case, he probably used a lot of self-control, and I know that to be part of his makeup. Whereas, I was very sentimental and emotional. I could cry easily and show my anger or despair. And yet again, insecurity, low self esteem, indecisiveness ruled my actions. I didn't have a soul-mate to discuss my fears and doubts, or sometimes excitement. No one to give me expert advice and opinions in my troubled days. Joyce had gone to Madrid. I didn't have close friends either at work or at the hostel. Even if I had opened my heart to someone, I might not have got the right advice. No one knew me or my circumstances well enough. So I was left to my own devices and intuitions, and my thoughts were causing a lot of turmoil in my head.

If it weren't for the divine intervention that I call Providence, goodness knows what action I would have taken and maybe regretted later. It was a good thing I didn't consult my roommates, those materialistic and good time girls who were after fast cars and fast men. They would change boyfriends like changing shoes. I still had a lot to learn. But for now, I couldn't possibly ignore the opportunity that came my way. I was not chasing anybody nor was it a snap decision. It took a lot of deliberation on my part and I am sure the same applied to him as well.

One day, when I was still at the hostel, the warden, Miss Evans, warned us girls at breakfast that we would have a visitor that evening before supper, and she said "Do try and look your best, she is Helen Temple, the beauty editor of WOMAN magazine". She was coming to show us how to use makeup properly. We were all ready and waiting when she arrived in an estate car bringing her reclining chair and all her paraphernalia. We made room for it in the centre of the lounge. Helen Temple was petite and blonde, well groomed, as you might expect from someone in her position. She had brought with her an array of beauty products to show us and introduced herself and the work she was doing. Then she asked for someone to be the guinea-pig for the demonstration. No one volunteered, they all wanted to watch and learn from her methods.

I wasn't really interested so it was left to me to sit in that chair. During the demonstration she was talking non-stop. I settled down, she adjusted the chair in a semi-reclining position, put a band on my head to hold my hair back, and she said "First we have to clean her face with a cleansing cream". She liberally applied some kind of lotion with a pad of cotton-wool with upward motions trying to wipe the dirt off my face. She was most surprised to see there wasn't any. "You have cleaned your face?" I replied, "No, I don't use makeup". Then, "It is remarkable that your skin is not dry. May I ask how old you are?" I said 29. She complimented me, then proceeded to put on various layers of foundation or whatever she called it. I shut my eyes. She was doing all sorts of things to my face, neck, eyes, eyebrows and eyelids. When she came to my lips, I asked her if she would mind if I did my lips myself. She let me use the lipstick while holding the mirror for me and was satisfied with the final result. That was the only thing I knew how to do.

Everyone was watching and asking questions for more information. Helen Temple wasn't there to enhance my beauty, she was there to sell her stuff for which she probably would get a commission, and also sell the magazine.

At great length, she emphasised the importance of a good cleansing cream such as product X and definitely a good foundation such as product Y and all the other make-ups and various cosmetics she used that evening, that according to her transformed my face.

She did good business and everyone was satisfied. There I was I all dolled up and nowhere to go. I didn't dare to let Krikor see me in that state.

After she had gone, the girls in the dining room were still discussing how well she transformed my face, and were delighted with all the stuff they bought from Helen Temple with a certain brand name they couldn't wait to try.

The next day when I came in from work there was a note for me on the notice board. "Would Miss Sarafian call the Woman magazine, Helen Temple wishes to speak to her." So, I rang. In short, she wanted me to do some modelling for the magazine. No, not clothes, just makeup, as she thought I had perfect skin and very good bone structure and was an ideal candidate for a makeover. I said I was sorry but I was at work all day and wouldn't have the time. She said they could arrange for the photographic sessions to be at the weekends. I told her I'd like to think about it. She also told me they were going to pay the going rate, which was very tempting.

The next evening when I saw Krikor I told him what had happened. At the time I was still working for Dunlop. He said "Definitely not". "But why? It will be fun." He was not amused. I didn't understand his reaction. He didn't think it appropriate for me to be all plastered up with makeup featured in the magazine for all the world to see. That was that.

I understood his mind. I was still a single girl not accountable to anybody. I was not yet known to the Armenian community as his particular friend. Bur he was very conscious of his own reputation and standing. He had pride and a dignity beyond words.

I was very disappointed and started having mixed feelings. I gave in grudgingly. I didn't want to call the Woman magazine myself, so I asked the office is they wouldn't mind ringing on my behalf and say "Miss Sarafian regrets but she is not interested". Helen Temple didn't take my "no" for an answer and called again, but I did not bother to reply. I regretted very much not accepting that offer, I would have enjoyed the experience.

Little did I know that some 48 years later I would be modelling for the WOMAN magazine, this time not just being made up by them, but also having a full makeover, hair, clothes, everything. They called me "A stunning grandmother" in their magazine, with a smiling picture that doesn't look like me. I hope I didn't offend the memory of my dear husband who was so opposed to the idea.

At the time I was upset and had some doubts about marrying him. Was he being masterly or authoritarian? I would have wished him to be more liberal. If this was the beginning of things to come, was I doing the right thing? I had had enough of being ordered about by my brother, I wanted to be liberated of all ties, to be my own woman. Was I looking for a "yes man", and was I perfect myself? And more importantly, would we be able to make it work? All these questions needed answers, and they would come in time.

It was early days yet, we were seeing each other quite often. One day, at an unexpected moment, he said "Would you like to help me sort out my bills, they are all over the place and I have to see the accountant shortly?" I hadn't done that kind of thing before so I asked him to show what he meant. I spent a weekend working on his books, getting them ready for the accountant to prepare the balance sheet. That was the start, and after that it was my duty to prepare the books, every year, for thirty years. I also became his receptionist on top of my other duties!

It wasn't very long before he realised I could help him every day. He just said one day, quite casually, "Instead of working at Dunlop why don't you work with me?" I was surprised. I said

"What do you mean?" I wasn't expecting such a question. Was he going to employ me? How could I take money from him, and if I didn't, how could I pay the hostel fees? He just said, as though he was reading my mind, "There is no need for you to go to work anymore. I think you had better give in your notice and we'll see where we go from there."

I reluctantly obliged, still not clear in my mind how I was going to live. I had never asked for money from anybody in my life and certainly, I couldn't expect him to pay me.

Two weeks later I had left my office job. Things gathered speed after that. Without my knowledge and to surprise me, he had spoken to his jeweller friend, Sdepan Aydinian, to make me an engagement ring. On his instructions I went to see this man in his Bloomsbury flat to collect the ring! Aydinian was a gregarious person, very talkative and a little loud. The ring was ready in a little red box. It was a diamond solitaire. He put it on my finger to make sure it fitted properly, and it did. It was a beautiful sparkling ring, but hardly a surprise gift anymore! When I brought back the precious ring he chose the right moment to put it on my finger solemnly and affectionately. There was no ceremony, no fuss, no company present. It was the first step of a contract between us that needed no elaborate demonstration to the outside world. I already knew the significance of that invaluable token, it closed all doors of doubt and uncertainty.

It was formal, we were engaged. I wasn't terribly excited and I wasn't dying to show my ring to the world. Which world? Only the girls at the hostel saw it that evening and I was congratulated warmly. It didn't make me feel any different. After all this time and heartbreaking episodes, it was expected. He wouldn't take his commitments lightly. Now we were betrothed the real story would soon follow.

It was time to take practical actions. Since leaving my job I was going to his surgery every day to do his errands and be his receptionist. We had not discussed anything about the wedding business yet. It was a subject we both avoided at the moment. Krikor had opened a current account at the local Post Office in my name with a tidy sum to start off with and it was up to me to withdraw what amount was needed for my or his household expenses. He was very busy working as usual and I was there to answer the phone or the door, and make the patients' appointments. Our weekends would start on Saturday afternoons when we could go out together. And every evening I was back at the hostel as usual. My parents were now reconciled to my situation, though they never asked any questions, but, I knew for sure that they were concerned as to how soon or whether we would get married. In one of my letters, I had told them we were waiting for the spring.

*   *   *   *

I had an acquaintance from Istanbul called Aghavni, in her 40s, who was temporarily staying with her married sister, Hrip Spencer, in Nottingham. Later on by coincidence she met and married a well-to-do Armenian gentleman called Mr. Tossounian, a well known personality in the community, who originally needed a live-in companion for his very old mother. Aghavni was outgoing, friendly and a good homemaker. The couple liked each other and it was a good match. In the early days of their marriage she used to feel very alone and isolated out in the country. Away from the city lights, and having no other acquaintance here but me at first, she often asked us to visit them at the weekends, usually on Sundays.

They had a Tudor-style house in Windsor and a very large garden with lots of fruit trees, much too quiet and isolated for someone as extrovert as Aghavni, who, as far as I remember, used to be the life and soul of any party. Utterly bored in that solitary confinement, she often invited people over, especially in the summer, when their garden was very enjoyable for folks like us, city dwellers. Mr. Tossounian used to grow all their vegetables; and the fruit trees like apple, plum, pear, cherry, walnut and other fruits provided enough to feed an army, but the guests were offered the windfalls only, unless they were special friends.

Occasionally we accepted their hospitality. Mr. Tossounian was a rather self-important person but he was always happy to see us, acknowledging perhaps Krikor's professional status to be an asset in his exclusive inner circle. We in turn, held him in respect. He had an aura of haughtiness which was intimidating for new comers.

While the men discussed community affairs, Aghavni and I used to sit separately, when she would tell me all about the latest news. We were both new in this environment and didn't know many people. But she had more occasions to meet them than I did. She revelled in gossiping about people who for me were just names. She knew some of the latest goings-on in others' homes, and she liked or disliked them according the reception she got from them. But, because she was now Mrs. Tossounian, as she often reminded me (in case I had forgotten), she very much enjoyed the flattery she received from new guests.

Aghavni was fun to be with. What she lacked in culture, she certainly made up with open hospitality. To visit her home was like an introduction. You met old and new people, and created your own circle. She made her garden in the summer a very attractive place to visit. For us, it was difficult to get there as we did not have a car. Krikor had put in an order for a Hillman a long time ago, and we were still waiting in the queue for its delivery. To go to Windsor, we had to take two buses, and the return journey was more of a bother as late-night transport was not very frequent.

Now that winter was upon us, serious plans had to be made. My brother announced that he and his wife were expecting their first baby in May. I was glad for them and for myself, as this meant Diran would not be hassling me any more. He was eagerly pursuing his career prospects. He now had an MA from Columbia University, and was applying for the post of assistant professorship.

Mr. Tossounian's old mother spoke only Turkish, and was pressing us to marry soon. "Şu kizin parmağina bir yüzük tak", she kept saying to Krikor, which means "put a ring on this girl's finger". She could not understand what we were waiting for. Come to think of it, I did not know what we were waiting for either.

Then, one day, after a long pause, he said he didn't think that his flat was suitable for a family. Unfortunately, he still had two years' lease unexpired. Besides the surgery and the waiting room on the ground floor, he had a bedroom on the first and shared a bathroom with another couple; and in the basement he had his workshop. The flat itself was not self-contained at all. There was no kitchen, and I used to put the kettle on a gas ring in the workshop where, on a shelf, assorted samples of grinning dentures were on display. He was worried that this accommodation would not suit me, and was forever apologetic, even though we were not yet married.

Had he married one of the girls from well-to-do families who had designs on him, he would have had to meet their high expectations. Whereas, I was a humble girl who had nothing and demanded nothing. Maybe, I was a bargain after all ...

One day when I arrived in the morning, Krikor was all smiles and looked happy. I thought, that's a change. I was curious. "What's happened, what's the matter?" He had asked the owner to give us another room to convert into a kitchen. The only possibility was one vacant maid's room in the basement near his workshop. It was a long, galley-shaped room, at the end there was a perfectly good bath and near the door a good scullery type stone sink. He would be charged extra for this makeshift bathroom-cum-kitchen, but it would be just ours, no sharing, and we did not mind. It sounds odd, but it was the best solution.

In the meantime, he still had a couple of years' lease, and until then, we had to make do with things as they were. Not that I was demanding, I had never had any place in my name before, and even though he was worried that it was not good enough for a new bride, I was not in the least bit bothered. What with sharing a bedroom and everything else with others for the past three years, I could put up with any arrangements.

CHAPTER 10 MARRIED LIFE

We were both ready to commit ourselves to each other and after the New Year, maybe towards the spring, we were thinking of contacting the Priest for a suitable date to get married. We were planning, but not necessarily rushing into things. Then the resident Vicar told Krikor on a Sunday after the service that the last date he could marry us before Lent was the 12th February, and by then, we ought to have got the civil marriage certificate from the Registrar's Office in Cheniston Gardens. Our Church had no official powers to issue a marriage certificate at the time.

We did not know how to go about these things. After more enquiries, Krikor found out that the date had to be booked well in advance. Since we were serious about it now, he took the next available date which was the 7th February, 1950. He needed two witnesses: he arranged all that. I would arrive early at the flat for our appointment that morning, where his friends were already waiting. A taxi took us to the red brick building near High Street Kensington where, without a big ceremony, we exchanged our vows and signatures, and he put the wedding ring on my finger for the first time and we were married in the eyes of the law. There was no excitement, no partying.

There was an official photographer at the door, who took a few shots, and that was it! It was a bright and cold day. Afterwards, we all went to a restaurant to quietly celebrate. Unfortunately, I had a nasty cold and we could not stay very long. I managed to survive the whole thing, which was very unemotional, but very significant all the same, and with a slight temperature and runny nose, I went back to bed at the Hostel straight away.

Just married – on the steps of Kensington Registry Office

When the girls saw me later on, they were aghast and thought the wedding had never happened. I showed them my ring, and said, "Yes, I am married now". They could not understand what I was still doing at the Hostel, rather than be with my husband. I explained to them, though they found it difficult to understand, that I would not consider myself properly married until the church wedding. This was to be a few days later, on Sunday, in the quaint little Church of Saint Sarkis in Iverna Gardens. Mr. Tossounian was our best man and Dr. Derounian, Krikor's friend from the American University of Beirut, gave me away. We had no relatives, not many friends either. In fact, Krikor did not want many people to know. No fuss, he hated to be the centre of attention. It was a strictly intimate gathering, consisting of the Tossounians and Derounians, the Deacon and Choir Master and their wives, and some girlfriends from the Hostel.

I have got some very good photographs of the day, me in full white wedding gown and long veil and a simple head-dress, holding a white bouquet of spring flowers, and Krikor, in his evening suit which I had had specially pressed the day before.

Afterwards, there was no reception, no party. Everybody went their own way and we returned home to change, while the limousine waited at the door to take us on honeymoon to an exclusive country hotel in Ascot that the Tossounians had arranged. Living so close in Windsor, they came to visit us a couple of days later.

At the altar in St Sarkis Church

I could not believe I was not Miss Sarafian any more. Having no one from my family at the Church was very sad for me. It would have been more meaningful had my aunt and uncle from Paris been present. But unfortunately, it could not be arranged. My new life would start as Mrs. Gorgodian and I should now have to get used to my new status as a married woman.

It was only about a fortnight before our big day that we had time to think about buying a couple of essential items. We needed a cooker, yes, but before that we needed a new bed. Krikor said, "I hate shopping, why don't you go to Barkers and order whatever you want?" I insisted that we should both go, as these were not items that could be returned if they did not suit. I said, "I'm not going alone."

Unfortunately, in 1950, all the shops closed on Saturdays at 1pm. So we had to go shopping in Krikor's lunch-hour.

Tentatively, I had visited Barkers, our local department store, and considered one or two possibilities. In those days, Barkers bedding and furniture departments were across the road from the main store; you could get to the department from the basement of the main store via an underpass. They had a huge selection on the second floor, which made it even more difficult to choose.

I said, "Once we have the bed, we must also get the bedding that goes with it, pillows, blankets, sheets, etc." But Krikor replied, "Look, I haven't got the time for all that, let's get the bed now and you carry on with the rest". He had to get back for the next patient. So in a hurry, we chose a bed and after he had gone, I was left alone to get all the rest to be delivered in the next few days.

I did not realise buying sheets and blankets was so complicated. I did not know the first thing about different qualities, shapes and sizes. Fortunately, I had help from a middle-aged motherly assistant. She was very happy to oblige. I was exhausted by the time I finished.

When we returned from our honeymoon, we gradually managed to get a few more pieces of furniture for my own clothes and belongings. We were settling down in slow steps. Through friends, we found a cleaning lady as I did not want to allow the housekeeper into our rooms. I still found shopping for food and cooking difficult. I preferred salads and grills or even a stew, which were not complicated, and I just about managed. I learned from my mistakes. Fortunately, Krikor was not fussy and was very patient. He knew I was trying to improve myself. We had a beautiful new gas cooker with a glass oven door, which suited me fine, because I could check if the food was done. We also had a small table and two chairs, so that it was nice and cosy in our little kitchen cum bathroom. At least it was ours, no sharing.

I was getting domesticated, little by little. I was also learning to be choosy when buying groceries or vegetables and fruit. It's a pity there were no supermarkets then. I hated to be extravagant, and I was very careful in spending money as I had the feeling I was using up Krikor's money and was worried about how I would tell him when the deposit in the account ran out. Never in my life had I been in this position. I still did not consider myself an equal partner with rights in money matters.

One day, Krikor found me counting out my change and writing down some figures. He asked me what I was doing, and realised I was embarrassed. "Are you short of money? Why didn't you tell me?" he asked. After this, he saw to it that with a joint account and cheque book, I would never worry about such things again. He tried to tell me that we shared everything, and that I was very much the mistress of the house. It was as difficult for him to share as it was for me, in different ways. For me, it was like being on probation, I was still new and had to prove myself.

Krikor started taking me to community events and introducing me to his friends with rather an obvious pride: "My wife, Anahid". He was known, among those who had met him often at those affairs, as a 'confirmed bachelor'. Later on, I heard through the grapevine that he had been a candidate for match-makers in some circles without his knowledge, and now there were a couple of disappointed souls around.

Gradually, the Gorgodians were being accepted at Court, the Armenian Court, that consisted of a dozen grandees who were the pioneers of the London Armenian Community Council, and before long, Dr Gorgodian was invited to join them. A decade later, when the Armenian House was created in 1962 and my husband was among the Trustees, one pompous self-important man, bulging with superiority, asked Mr. Benlian (the main benefactor and founder), "Why did you get that Tashnak into Hai Doon?" - meaning my husband. (A Tashnak is an Armenian with nationalistic political beliefs.) To which Mr. Benlian replied, within the hearing of another Big Head, "If all Tashnaks were like Dr. Gorgodian, I'd become a Tashnak myself."

At the Hilton

In Mr. Benlian's Turkish, that would be, "Eğer bütün Taşnaklar Doktor gibi olursa bende Taşnak olurum". Thank-you, Mr. Benlian, may God bless your soul. He knew he could not have chosen a better advocate and devotee of the Armenian House.

Krikor loved and breathed Hai Doon. That was his second home, and he spent a lot of his spare time working for it, not only sitting on committee chairs, like some, but also turning his hand to practical tasks, like mending fuses, unblocking drains, going onto the roof to check for leakages and any other menial tasks for which a resident odd job man would have been required. He had learnt all those skills while at university during holidays, working as an apprentice for people in the building trade, like plumbers, electricians and carpenters, for pocket money. He said with pride, "I've also worked for a tailor for a week, and I can even sew on buttons!"

Mr. Benlian often dropped in on us informally, without waiting for a meeting, when we lived in Cheniston Gardens on the opposite corner to the Armenian House. The two men would discuss important matters over a glass of whisky. He used to park his old Bentley in front of our house. He was very fond of that old car, he would not exchange it for a newer model. Old-fashioned maybe, but it was reliable and comfortable.

After his beloved wife, Shoushanig died, he was inconsolable. At the wedding of our daughter, Sonia, in 1972, he came to Church (All Saints, in St. John's Wood) but declined our invitation to the reception in the De Vere Hotel, Kensington. I had to persuade him by saying that there would be no dancing or music, just a friendly party with food and drink. He looked at me, and said "I'll do it for the Doctor". And come he did, and was very happy to have done so. I could see he was enjoying himself with people he knew and associated with.

The same applied to Dr. Derounian, who had lost his wife, the lovely Kitty, the previous year. He was persuaded to come too. We were very old friends and had much in common, and their daughter, Zabelle, was also our god-child.

There was an established core of good people who were the guardians of this community. Things were unchanged until the influx of a large number of Armenians - from Cyprus to begin with, to be followed by those from other near-Eastern Countries like Iran, Lebanon, Iraq etc. They all came for their own safety and security, like the rest of us had done before them. And thus, London became the melting-pot of our community in the Diaspora. They came in waves bringing their own distinct traits, their particular customs, and the amalgamation of dogmas started to challenge the harmony of a once-united community.

At first, we had many teething problems that, after a while, were ironed out by goodwill. Most people had honest nationalist convictions, but some were fanatical and did more harm than good. In the end, we had to learn to live with each other with respect and tolerance. Even now, occasionally, the Armenian Vesuvius erupts, lashing out hot ashes that cause damage to our unity which is more important than separatist doctrines. We are a handful of Armenians compared with our enemies. Our pitiful marches on April 24th with a couple of hundred like-minded people are negligible when you compare them with other nationals' demonstrations that paralyse the high streets. When are we going to learn to get organised properly?

*   *   *   *

I got carried away again and skipped a few years since the days we got married. We spent two years in Wetherby Gardens in the beginning of our life together. Before the birth of my brother's baby, we realised we were expecting our first baby too. When it was confirmed, Krikor was over the moon. I used to catch him sometimes with a faint smile and a new expression on his face, as if he wanted to say something but was just content thinking about it. Several times a day, he would ask me if I was feeling all right. To me, it made no difference. I could not even believe I was going to be a mother. He was more excited than I was.

I was not prepared for motherhood, just as I was not prepared to be a housewife. In six months' time, our life was going to change, and Krikor was afraid I was not going to be able to cope alone. The seriousness of this new responsibility still had not dawned on me. I was not counting the days, and if I did, I would probably have panicked. The birth was still quite a long way off.

No one, no female close friend or family member, or nurse, spoke to me about conception, labour, birth, feeding and changing babies, about the layette and nappies, sleepless nights, bathing and comforting the baby, or all those experiences that are the alphabet of motherhood from pregnancy to the caring of your offspring. I was ignorant of the needs of that little creature inside me, and was unaware of the realities waiting for me, until I was showing physical signs on my abdomen and felt the first kick from inside that took me by surprise. Sometimes, it was so strong that it worried me in case something was wrong. At those times, Krikor would just put his hand on my tummy and smile and laugh and look so happy. He wanted to be a father so very badly!

As I was needing not only advice but also guidance, I turned to Kitty who had already had her first child. The Derounians were both very helpful. He was our doctor and she was a nurse. I was immediately checked in at the Princess Beatrice Hospital, the nearest to us, and had regular appointments arranged. The baby was due at the end of November, and we couldn't wait! I had no idea what to do or what not to do, what to eat or not, or whether I needed to take any supplements. Being anaemic, I was prescribed iron tablets and some other vitamins. I was very healthy, and did not think I needed anything else, but was told all this was for the good of the baby. I was determined I was going to do everything right.

My brother's wife had had a baby boy, and they called him Lawrence (Larry). My family knew of my news, and I was getting good wishes from everywhere. I was getting heavier and heavier, and found going up and down three flights of stairs difficult. I definitely needed someone to help me. I thought of my aunt in Paris, Mo (short for "Morakouyr", literally mother's sister). She was free and unattached and could come, but needed a visa, not being a French subject. She needed a formal invitation. After completing the applications process, she was granted a visa for three months in order to help her niece during pregnancy. We arranged her arrival to be two months before the birth, leaving one month after - the most difficult time for me. I was very happy when she came, she was so good and helpful.

Fortunately, my husband and Mo got on very well together. He called her Mo too. She could not do enough for me, even though she was no longer young herself. Daida, my uncle, was left alone in the flat in Paris, but he could manage to look after himself. Fortunately, Mo could speak English. In her home town of Adapazar in Turkey, where she was born and brought up in a wealthy family, she received a good education at an American missionary school. She remembered enough of the language to get by and even do my shopping. She also cooked for us and became indispensable. The last days before the birth, I was very uncomfortable, everything was becoming an effort, especially those unending carpeted stairs, as I was afraid of tripping.

CHAPTER 11 BECOMING PARENTS

The time came for me to be admitted to hospital. After a long, dry labour, without much medical help - the gas and air didn't work - and in great agony, I gave birth to a beautiful little baby girl of 7 pounds and 10 ounces. After she was born and wrapped, she was put in my arms. "Oh God! You gave me this little angel, I am so grateful." I was in heaven. That little bundle was warm and soft, with minuscule fingers and a funny little face. I could not stop looking at her in amazement and wonder. She made me forget all the pain she had caused me. She was just perfect. Tiny mouth yawning, eyes closed and a worried look on her face, as if to say "Why did you disturb me, I was so happy where I was! I want to sleep."

I cuddled and cradled her, and sang her a song, a tune that came to my head; it was our tune. I sang to her softly, kissing her gently and loving her with all my being.

They used to take the babies away after every feed and I did not want to let her go. When Krikor was told on the phone that he had a baby daughter, he could not come to the hospital fast enough. They gave him the little bundle to hug, and he had tears in his eyes he did not want me to see. He too started talking to her in whispers and kissed her gently. He said to me, "Thank you for giving me this treasure." Our baby had two loving parents; we were both captivated.

Of course, it was only just the beginning. The nurses were doing all the hard work themselves! Soon, I would be left to do all that alone. I was kept in hospital for two weeks. I was not at all happy there. The staff nurse was rude to me; not only could she not pronounce my name properly, but she also used to make fun of it.

I did not want to complain in case she would somehow harm my baby. We could not see what they did to our babies when they took them away from us. I did not want them to take it out on her. My little angel would be at their mercy, so I kept quiet and did not complain.

I decided to bottle-feed her, that way I could see how much milk she had taken. Sometimes, she would not wake up and missed her feed, but the nurses would still take her away and if on waking she was hungry and cried, they let her cry a long time until the next feed and there was nothing I could do except cry too.

At last, the time came to take her home. Her new cot was ready, with all her new bedding: pillows, and sheets and blankets. We bought everything from Daniel Neal, the baby shop on High Street Kensington. All her nappies were terry towelling and Harrington gauze; there were no disposable nappies in those days. Krikor came in a taxi to collect the baby and me. Even though I had complained about the hospital, at least everything had been done for me there.

Fortunately, I did not have to worry about shopping and food initially, Mo was looking after all that. My job was to take care of the baby and her needs. And it was time consuming! I had no time for myself, sometimes I just stayed in my nightie, I did not have time to change. The baby was a slow sucker, and many times in the night I had to get up to give her a bottle that half-way through she would abandon to fall back asleep. I was so tired, I could not always wake up when she cried, and sometimes Krikor would have to feed her. Just how such a little thing could transform your life is unbelievable. I was like a zombie during the day, I wanted to sleep the whole time.

Gradually, things would get into a routine and it would be easier to follow a timetable. The baby was gaining weight steadily and getting prettier. I could not keep my eyes off her when feeding, she was so funny. I was hoping she would pass the stage when she fell asleep during feeding. If only she would not wake up at night. I can't remember at what point the night calls got less and less. Sometimes, she would sleep for long stretches and, Hallelujah!, we would have slept a whole uninterrupted night.

Sometimes when changing and feeding her she would smile at me and how pleased I used to be that she recognised me. Until the health visitor told me that it was a sign of "wind".

Each morning as part of our routine, I used to put the baby in her pram, cover her well from head to toe and leave her in the little private garden we had at the back of the house in front of the surgery. There was a huge communal garden which all surrounding residents could access, and we could let ourselves into it by just pushing our gate. My baby was safe in our little patch as her father could keep an eye on her through the French windows.

We called our baby, Anna; that was the name most of my English friends called me; it was short and easy and also was Armenian as well as English. The Tossounians became her godparents. We had a christening service in the little Saint Sarkis Church where we were married, and Father Bessak Toumayan, who had become our new Vicar, officiated. She did cry a lot when immersed in the water - but then most babies do not like being put in water by someone they do not know, who has a black beard and is chanting down at them at the same time, "Havadk, houys yev ser" - Faith, Hope and Love,

As soon as she was out of the water, I quickly patted her dry and put her in warm clothes and comforted her with my hugs. How I loved her! Is there a higher, stronger love than a mother's?

Unfortunately, Mo had gone back to Paris, her permit had expired. She took the overnight sleeper train. How I missed her afterwards. Now my time was taken totally with motherhood duties, plus the usual chores. There were not enough hours in the day. When the surgery hours ended on Saturday at 1pm, I could relax a little bit. The phone and the doorbell no longer rang and it was just us three: daddy, mummy and baby. We were quite content in our little world that was complete. We used to take the baby to the Park, and prop her up in her pram to watch the ducks in the pond. The pigeons and the sparrows would circle above her head, and she would squeal with delight, looking at those flying creatures while she did "dzapig dzapig" (clapping) and stretching her little arms towards them. She had gorgeous big black eyes with thick long eyelashes, rosy cheeks and the loveliest toothless smile.

Fortunately, the winter was over now and we could leave her out longer in our little garden. I could also push the pram to the shops. Soon, teething problems started and we suffered those pains with her. We were rewarded by her first "dadda, mamma", words that sent her father to seventh heaven. She was bright and happy.

That first summer, my mother came to visit for three months and adored her grand-daughter. Our visits to the Tossounians became less and less, as it was difficult for us to travel to Windsor with a baby and carry-cot, on and off buses. Our car had not yet been delivered.

After her short visit, my mother left us to go back to Istanbul via Paris to stay with Mo. In the meantime, we started making new friends in our community. We could not easily visit people as it was inconvenient for us. Therefore, we had an open house for close friends like Major Fred Harris and his wife, Peggy, Krikor's army friends from Rangoon. Peggy was a nurse and she used to baby-sit for us occasionally. Also, there was Beatrice, a pianist from Baghdad, who used to come round quite often. Then there was Hayguhi, a girl from Istanbul, who had been here even before the war staying with her aunt; she later became a very close friend. There was another single girl, Seta Izmitlian, who was a nurse staying with her uncle who was a well-known personality within the Community. She often dropped in when she had time off. I was not isolated any more, and these were people who knew my situation and were supportive. It was a pity I had not known them previously, before my marriage, when I had been agonising over what to do and did not have a close friend to pour my heart out to.

My friend Joyce had already left London by that point. She had gone to Madrid to work for the Foreign Office. She was a very capable girl, and married an English colleague from work. They came to London to get married at Southwark Cathedral, and returned to Madrid to settle in their own home. I think very highly of Joyce as a loyal friend. We still correspond regularly, and see each other whenever she comes to visit London, usually in the summer. She was recently awarded an MBE by the Queen for her services to the British community in Madrid.

*　　　　*　　　　*　　　　*

When Anna was 19 months old, in the summer of 1952, we decided to take a family holiday. Krikor left all the arrangements to me. I have always loved islands and was curious about the Channel Islands. I chose Jersey, not so far by air. So I booked our holiday from an advert, a fortnight in a hotel in Jersey, full-board and inclusive of flight, returning late August.

The Channel Islands Terminus used to be in High Street Kensington, probably where Safeway is now. So it was easy for us to get to the airport bus with luggage and pushchair. It was so close we were there in no time. At the other end of our journey, the owner was waiting to take us in his car to the Hotel which was near a small farmhouse with a few cows and chickens. So we always had fresh eggs, cream and farm produce, all organic.

We were not far from the sea, and used to spend a lot of time on the beach. It was an ideal holiday. Anna loved the sea, and played with her bucket and spade on the sands. We enjoyed every minute of our time there. Two weeks passed very quickly, and we returned to a cooler and rainy London. Back to the grind-stone.

I had bought Anna some colourful picture books, and before she could even speak she recognised all the names of colours and flowers and all the domestic animals, the birds and the butterflies. She learnt to say "gadou, shounig, touchoun, titenik" (cat, puppy, bird, butterfly) and "moo" for the cow. When she had new red shoes, she loved the "gamiy goshig". If I gave her a sweet she would want "eegou had" (two). I remember everything she did or said as if it were yesterday.

Until we expected our second child, Anna had all our attention and priority in everything. Our world revolved around her, but we tried very hard not to spoil her, though it was not always easy not to. I think we were trying to keep up with the Derounians; they had their second child and we were expecting ours. Our accommodation wasn't suitable for a big family, but fortunately the lease would soon expire.

CHAPTER 12 MOVING HOME

Our biggest problem now was to find accommodation suitable for Krikor's clinic as well as for the rest of the family. I wanted a garden for the sake of the children, and he wanted to buy a place that used to belong to a dentist for practical reasons. Locality was also important. We spent months looking for a house that fulfilled all our requirements. I viewed lots of houses with lovely gardens but they were too far from public transport, which was a drawback.

We even went to look at a house in Harley Street. Krikor wanted that very much but the lease was very short, there was no garden and the rooms were most inconveniently arranged, with kitchen downstairs, living room upstairs, bedroom on the top floor and surgery on the ground floor. With two babies I would be running up and down all day and there was nowhere to put the pram and the pushchair. And on top of all those inconveniences it was atrociously expensive. Obviously it was not meant to be a family home, it was more suitable for sharing with another professional, though the famous "Harley Street" name was a draw. It could have worked had we separated our home life from the business. That would have been a glorified luxury at the expense of our new found happiness. It was unthinkable.

In the meantime, Krikor was checking advertisements in the Dental Journal and it was there that we found our next home and practice combined for sale by a retiring dentist. 29 Cheniston Gardens, just off High Street Kensington and between two splendid parks was an ideal location and we would stay there for 29 years.

29 Cheniston Gardens has the Gorgodian Family history written all over the internal walls. That's where we were living when we had our youngest daughter, Michèle; where both my parents came to live with us for 15 years and died within a year of each other; where our middle daughter, Sonia, got married and gave us two grand-children, a girl and a boy; and where all our daughters became University graduates.

It was also at 29 Cheniston Gardens that my beloved husband was diagnosed with cancer. He suffered for three years, deteriorating all the time. I even went to Lourdes expecting a miracle. It wasn't to be.

All my relatives and friends from abroad, especially from the States, came to stay with us. My school friend Norma, who lived in Los Angeles, was a regular visitor. She would just write and say "I am coming", sometimes with family and friends. My cousin, Knar, came a few times. So did my brother, several times, alone or with the entire family, all eight of them. When my parents were living with us as well, believe me, it was not easy to create extra sleeping accommodation for eight at short notice. That was in 1959, when he had six children and I had three. With six adults and nine children between the ages of one and nine, the place was chaotic.

Diran, my dear brother, had just received a Fellowship of Science from the University of Florida to conduct mathematical research in Numerical Analysis at the University of Rome. He had been a professor of Maths in Michigan and Florida, to be followed by Utah and finally New Orleans. He had written umpteen articles, thesis, books; he was invited from all over the world to give lectures, including London, Oxford, Germany, Denmark and Moscow, and many more. His methods had been used by NASA in the process of re-entry of spacecraft and satellites in Lunar Expeditions. Currently, at the ripe old age of 89, he is trying to finish his latest book on yet more mathematical analysis. His mind is still very sharp. All his life he was dedicated to solving Maths problems that were beyond the comprehension of ordinary Maths scholars. He has tutored hundreds of students many of whom have become professors themselves. He has suffered in his private life, with the death, first of his only son and eldest child, Larry, who had just qualified as a medical doctor, then of his beloved wife Dorothy, through medical misadventure after a complicated operation, and recently of one of his daughters, Susy, in a traffic accident. Even though he survived all those personal tragedies, his health suffered in many ways. Now he has only four lovely daughters, Dorothy, Carolyn, Wendy and Miriam, and grandchildren he loves dearly. His daughters are always around to take care of their brilliant father. We often speak on the phone. I love him dearly, my precious, beloved, unique brother, without whom I dare not think what would have happened to me and my parents.

Diran's wife, Dorothy, and daughters

29 Cheniston Gardens, only two doors away from the Armenian House, was the centre of many a meeting, whether my husband's or mine. Well before the Armenian House was ready to open its doors as our Community Centre, our house had been used as Sunday School, every Sunday for two years with three volunteer lady teachers. Dozens of children used to attend, to learn how to read and write in Armenian. That is where the Sunday School of our Community started before moving to Armenian House, until the numbers grew and grew and eventually the school settled where it has been since, using the premises of Reynold's High School in Acton with the financial help of Mr. Kevork Tahta's generous donation, under the patronage of the Church Council.

The vicinity of the two houses, ours and Hai Doon (Armenian House), was the reason why my husband and I were as involved in community affairs as we were. It was convenient. We became unofficial guardians of the Armenian House. We were always there for practical support whenever it was needed for various casual necessities. My husband was always available for advice and guidance to the resident secretaries to iron out any problems for the uneventful running of the Armenian House (A.H.). In fact, he was the best representative the Directors could have. Nothing was too much trouble for him. He gave his services unconditionally and with devotion. He simply loved the A.H. After his death I was invited to join the Board of Trustees, to serve in his place, and also as a liaison between them and the Ladies Committee, of which I was Chairman. It was an honour that I accepted with deep appreciation and humility, an obligation that I didn't take lightly. Also, to me, to belong to that noble establishment is more than a responsibility; it is, I feel, my husband's legacy, to cherish as he did, to serve as long as I am able to.

After being cramped in Wetherby Gardens in four separate rooms on three different floors with a kitchen-bathroom, an odd and impractical accommodation, moving to Cheniston Gardens and being the owners, by contrast, of a five storey house with thirteen rooms, all empty and all ours, was suddenly like acquiring wings of freedom; it was unbelievable! How could we use all that space? In actual fact all Krikor wanted was a surgery, a waiting room and a workshop for his practice. The first floor had three rooms; we converted the smallest one into a kitchen-dining room and used the other two as living room and bedroom. We had two more floors upstairs that I didn't want to use. They stayed empty for the time being. I had two children under three who needed all my attention; in addition I also had to help my husband with his patients' reception as much as I could. That meant running up and down all day long and making sure the children were safe too.

We had a boiler room in the basement where the water was being heated by a stove, burning coal day and night, and in the next room Krikor had his workshop fitted. There was also a scullery where we had our washing machine installed. This was a typical Victorian house, solid and old fashioned.

The most practical and most used and popular room in the whole house was our kitchen-dining room on the first floor. It was the hub of our family; we were always there cooking, eating, talking and looking out of the French windows which opened onto a balcony. We had a good view of what was going on outside; the tourists coming in coach loads to the hotel opposite. And when the Armenian House started in 1962, we had the whole community passing by our door, especially on Sundays after the

Church service, when it seemed the whole congregation was surging there, and it was getting full to capacity.

Our second daughter was born when we were still in Wetherby Gardens. On June 19, 1953, Coronation year. We called her Sonia. She was a lovely baby, very bubbly and with dark curly hair. She was lucky to have an elder sister, and when she was a bit older and on her feet, she was always following Anna and talking to her in her baby language. We couldn't understand it but Anna could and she used to translate it for us. The two girls were inseparable, they played together all day until Anna started to go to a nursery school later on. I was fully occupied all day long and when my husband finished his surgery he would come up to relax and have fun and games with the children. In a way he was lucky; he didn't have to go out to work and he was happy to know that his family was upstairs safe and secure.

Mo used to come at least once a year. She used to enjoy being with us and was a great help with baby sitting, doing our sewing and mending, making the girls some dresses and lending me a hand occasionally with the ironing. When she first came to our new house, she crossed the road and stood on the pavement opposite and gazing at our home, sizing it up and down, she named it "Gorgodian Palace". We had a few laughs and jokes on the new title but it stuck.

It was a happy home most of the time, very lived in and busy. The two top floors were unoccupied for a while until we had visitors, like Mo and Daida, and we expanded on to the second and third floors when my parents came and then we had our third daughter. Now the whole house with all the floors and rooms were fully occupied. Suddenly we didn't have an empty corner anymore.

Clockwise from left: Baba, Daida, Mayrig, Mo, Anna and Sonia

Daida was a regular visitor too. He used to take the Newhaven -
Dieppe route because he loved the long sea journey. He was
retired now and being an amateur painter, all our walls were
covered with his beautiful, unsophisticated paintings. He wasn't
exactly a Turner or a Van Gogh, but he had a realistic touch and
a quality of candid observation, like an unpolished diamond that
needs an expert hand to round the corners and put life into the
scene. Considering he had never had any lessons and was just
following his natural talent, we appreciated his work, such as of
the Sacré Coeur and Uriage les Bains, his beloved spa. My
favourite is the picture of their flat in Paris, their living room
complete with their cosy stove where they burnt logs of wood and
the smoke went up through pipes to the chimney and out of the
roof, and with their dresser, the dining table with the green table
cloth and his divan in the corner where he slept. Mo used the only
bedroom in the flat. They had a small kitchen and a washroom.
Their flat was very snug and comfortable, heated with radiators as
well as the stove, as Daida liked a really warm room where he

could sit in his shirt sleeves, and smoke his gauloise and drink his coffee or his plonk with his dinner. He knew he shouldn't do any of those things; the doctor had ordered him to stop smoking and drinking, but Daida wasn't a disciplined man, he did not take any notice of warnings and continued using his cheap luxuries until the day they finished him off.

When we had our third daughter, our family was complete; we had our three graces. Another beautiful, healthy girl, she was the biggest baby, over eight pounds, and she didn't look like a new born. I gave her formula SMA milk on Kitty's recommendation, which was supposed to be the nearest to human milk. She thrived on it and in no time I was giving her solids which I made at home myself and a mashed banana every day. She used to lap it up, and became a big, healthy baby. Now I was an expert mother, having practised on the other two, and with two older sisters to learn from, Michèle had no difficulty in developing faster than the others. She learnt their nursery rhymes, their songs, and when she was eighteen months old she was humming one of the French songs they were singing at school. Because she was too young to say the words "Dort, dort, l'enfant dort, l'enfant dormira bien vite" she just hummed the whole thing to the right tune. I was amazed, I couldn't believe my ears. I had never seen a child that age being able to sing so accurately. Later on when she too started taking piano lessons, after the others had given it up, she did very well in her exams, and with her teacher's recommendation she went for an interview at the Royal College of Music and was admitted to the junior department at the age of eleven.

I had a full house, as I said before, but I also had to think about feeding my crowd. Besides the occasional guests we were four adults and three growing children. Shopping was done almost every day. My father and I would go round the shops in High Street Kensington for bread, meat or fish, vegetables and fruit, for two families, my parents and us. My mother had her own kitchen and did her own cooking. She used to give me a list and I had my own. Most things were bought at Sainsbury's which wasn't a supermarket then, and I had to queue separately for every item at a different counter. The very first supermarket in the High Street came a few years later and was called Gardners, which later on became Safeways. Others like the Food Forum followed soon. It was so much easier to help yourself and be choosy. It was a novelty to put your hand on everything without being told "do not touch". Without realising it, one would buy more than intended.

I am sure the house in Cheniston Gardens kept me agile and fit. There was no need to go to a gym, I was doing my exercises going up and down the stairs and never getting tired. I was young and slim and on top of my housekeeping duties I used to watch over my children like a hawk and supervise their homework, not doing it for them, but seeing to it that it was done without too much television. Our daughters were very lucky to have both parents at home all the time. They were never neglected, nor experienced separation. I didn't feel the need to have a life of my own, to have a career or take up a hobby. There was no time for such things and it didn't ever occur to me to have a change.

On holiday in Worthing

My husband had his life downstairs in his clinic and he didn't like a lot of noise coming from upstairs. After all it was a professional house and we ought to preserve that status. He used to have some important patients, including foreign diplomats: Bulgarians, Turks, Greeks, French ... they all had great respect for him. Even the Turkish consul, who used to call him "Doktor Bey", was a regular patient. We used to get a lot of diplomatic personnel, all very satisfied customers.

Besides the great and the good, we had patients from all walks of life. My duties were to answer the door and the phone, let the newcomer into the waiting room and let Krikor know who had just arrived and also to make appointments and answer all queries. Looking back, just remembering those happy times when I didn't know what it meant to waste time or get bored, I wonder, was it really me turning the wheel of that production almost single handed? I only had one cleaning lady twice a week, two hours each time, for the whole house, and the very inconsistent and occasional help from my aged mother for a few years. My whole life was devoted to my family: my husband, my children, my parents. My own person was at the bottom of the list.

CHAPTER 13 LIFE AT GORGODIAN PALACE

After they arrived in 1954, my parents took a long time to get used to our way of life in London. My father was better at it, he used to go out every day to find his way around, but my mother never risked leaving the house unless it was to go to Church or the Armenian House if there was a talk or a lecture. Fortunately these places were all next door, well almost. She used to read a lot, and having time on her hands, all she wanted was to sit and chat with me about things and people she had left behind, her friends and neighbours. She was very homesick for a long time; unfortunately I didn't have the time for idle gossip and those people she mentioned I didn't remember or care about. My time was precious, I couldn't waste it on unimportant matters. History repeats itself. When now, I occasionally talk to my daughters about things that have nothing to do with our family and it's about people they don't know, they are not in the least interested. They are all so busy, they just haven't the time for detailed and trivial accounts. The only time I have their full attention is when I am unwell or there is urgent business I cannot deal with myself, and of course, they will do my shopping and do my errands too difficult for me to handle. When I am ill, they'll drop everything to be by my side. They are generous and caring children, bless them. But, once in a while one needs humdrum trivialities to make you forget the seriousness of an ordinary unglamorous life.

Sure, I can talk to my friends, some very intimate; we tell each other things, little grumbles and a little bit of gossip, the harmless kind of course, but not what you choose to tell your children. They are different things altogether. How I wish that my mother was here now and I could talk about things that we both find pleasure in, to our hearts content. I would sympathise with her now.

If it weren't for the Armenian papers from abroad that my husband used to get and those that Bessak Serpazan used to give to my father, I don't know what my parents would have done. Those newspapers were their lifeline. They devoured everything in detail from cover to cover and were aware of what went on in Armenian life in other countries. My father, whom we called Baba, used to make himself useful, stoking the fire for the boiler, taking the children to the park or nursery school.

The children all started by going to the private nursery nearby. Anna was three and a half when I first took her. In Kensington everything was very expensive, but we both wanted to give our children the best education that money could buy. Anna wasn't at all happy at first. I went to speak to the headmistress. She complained to me that Anna couldn't understand the simplest instructions like "sit down" or "shut the door". I was afraid that was the reason why she didn't want to go, because she couldn't communicate with them. All she knew was Armenian; that's what we spoke at home. With a little help from us she managed to learn some simple words in English and in no time she was keeping up with the others and telling us each day what she had learnt.

A year later when she was five, I took her to Allendale, the nearby fee-paying primary school where she stayed till she was eleven. Whatever Anna did or wherever she went, the other two followed her. When it was Sonia's turn to go to the primary school at five years old, we had just had our youngest daughter, Michèle, and in time she went down the same path as her elder sisters.

When Anna did her 11+ examination, she applied for a place in Godolphin & Latymer, a top grammar school in Hammersmith. She had to go for an interview first, so I went with her. While they took Anna in, I was left behind in the large assembly hall, waiting with the other parents. One of the staff, a Miss X, came to ask me a few questions that I found very odd. "Who are the Armenians? What kind of race and religion do they belong to? Where did we come from and why were we here?" I thought those were such absurd and offensive questions 40 years ago, and I doubt they would dare ask them nowadays. If they were asking me such things, I wondered what they were asking Anna inside. I was astonished but answered politely, "We are white, as you can see, we are Christian and belong to the Armenian Church in Kensington. My husband is a professional man and served in the British Army in Burma as Captain". She went away satisfied. I only hoped that Anna wouldn't be penalised at school for not being "one of them". A couple of years later Sonia joined her at Godolphin. This time the questions were more relaxed.

Anna was very good at languages, and went on to study them at University, where she graduated with an Honours Degree. From 1962 to 1975, I attended all the PTA meetings for my three daughters, starting from Anna's first year through to Michèle's last year at Godolphin and Latymer. Mrs Mason, their history teacher and deputy head, used to welcome me at all those events, and on the very last evening she shook my hand and said "Mrs. Gorgodian, you deserve a medal, you never missed a PTA in all those years, you must be a very caring mother". I left with sadness. An important chapter was closed. This bus route will never again be taken by my daughters. From eleven year olds they grew to be intelligent, highly educated and refined girls. I can only repeat with Mr. Blair, "Education, education, education!" Godolphin and Latymer School was a first class educational establishment. It is a pity it stopped being a grammar school and became an independent school, though still maintaining its very high standard.

When she left school, Sonia spent a year at London University, studying Maths, but she left to get married. However she did not give it up altogether. A few years later, when her first child was two years old, she took it up again with the Open University by correspondence and got her degree by working at night, shortly after the birth of her second child. Following a spell in teaching in a comprehensive school, she gave it up, disappointed at the system and instead worked with a firm where she gained work experience. She is now a successful marketing manager.

While still at school, after getting her 'O' and 'A' levels, Michèle still hadn't made up her mind about which University to apply to. Then she learned about American universities and their entrance examinations, made enquiries and went for it. After passing with the required grades she was admitted to Wellesley College in Massachusetts in 1977, reading Economics and French. She then graduated with a BA in December 1979 and came home to find her father wasn't well. She had a great shock as we hadn't told her.

Krikor was under observation, attending hospital for therapy. He had now reduced his workload and was semi-retired. We had good days and bad. It wasn't easy for any of us; he was suffering as a result of the treatment, feeling weak and ill.

Michèle found work in the City, but in 1982 decided she wanted to go to Australia and work there. Naturally I was very upset, begged her to reconsider. It was no use. She had made up her mind; she had already written to friends out there and was going to stay with them at first, in Sydney.

I was very cross, I threatened never to write to her. She broke my heart; but I had to give in. I had no right to stand in her way. After a few tears and sulks I let her go with my blessings. Michèle corresponded frequently, telling me about the life over there. She had found a job at the Banque Nationale de Paris as a financial analyst and stayed there for a year and a half.

In 1983, I noticed an article on the INSEAD Business School in France, and I sent this to Michèle as I thought she might be interested in applying there to do a Masters in Business Administration (MBA). The deadline for return of the application form was imminent. She immediately completed it and sent it in. That was the best thing that could have happened to her and to me. She secured an interview and was accepted. My daughter came back, but only to go away again, though this time not very far. She pursued her ambition, and rented a tiny house which she called "Diddy House". A year later she got her MBA from INSEAD and never looked back. In recent years, she has started her own consulting business and now works for a range of corporate clients.

Sonia's daughter, Georgia, is happily married and has just had her first child. Sonia's son, Daniel, who is 22, is doing his final year at the Royal Northern College of Music in Manchester.

While I can repeat the new mantra of Education etc. with conviction, I am slightly pessimistic at the prospect of those university graduates. A degree is the result of hard work and is an expensive luxury, but, maybe it is also a gamble. Like everything else you need luck. You have to be in the right place at the right time, take the opportunity in both hands. Some manage to be successful and make a fortune with just a mediocre education, with no qualification. With special skill and a flair for knowing how to turn things to their benefit, they succeed in life where graduates can't.

My husband worked very hard in his chosen profession. He was a first class dental surgeon, extremely conscientious, and very gentle, especially with children, who, though terrified, were at ease the minute they sat in his chair. He would dispel their fears. He gave every one of his patients the same excellent treatment although he did not have the latest eye catching gadgets or a flashy manner. He didn't believe in flattery, and he had no time for snobs. People trusted him. Some of his patients came from as far as Scotland, Somerset and a particular foreign diplomat even used to phone from Paris for an appointment before flying over. He was an extremely smart, good looking gentleman who used to bring me exquisite perfumes every time, either Arpège by Lanvin or Miss Balmain. I would be very embarrassed and thank him with confusion. He used to say, "Mrs. Gorgodian, it is my pleasure and I have chosen them specially for you. I don't think I could give your husband perfumes, could I?" He said he was grateful to our neighbour, another French attaché, who recommended us to him, after his dentist in Paris made a mess of his teeth. Once he had been treated by my husband he wouldn't trust anybody else.

Krikor's integrity was beyond question whether in the capacity of his profession or as a member of the Armenian community, sitting on various committees. Even at home, with me alone, he never criticised anyone or tolerated me doing it. If I ever repeated an unfavourable remark or gossip, or a hurtful comment, he would immediately come to the defence of that person and shut me up by saying, "What would you do in his place?" Sometimes he used to infuriate me. He would just say, "We don't know the whole truth" and that would be the end of that. He was kind, tolerant and just. I know, I became a better person after marrying him. I used to call him my 20th century saint. He was my guru and my role model.

Years ago, in the early fifties, one day the doorbell rang. It was Hovhannes Chalikian, well-known in the community, with a young woman holding a tatty suitcase. He said to my husband, "Doctor, this girl is homeless, she comes from Istanbul. You must give her a place to stay." How can anyone say that kind of thing to us, just because we did have the room, without asking us first if it is possible, or, even, please? I was speechless. But my husband had not only a good name but also a good heart. He couldn't refuse. After all he was put on the spot. All we knew about the girl was her name, Koharig. We were not told why she was homeless, who she really was and why she was here anyway. She didn't like being questioned, she pretended to be very upset.

We took her in not even knowing how long this arrangement was for. We gave her a clean bed, board and lodging, without expecting anything in return. After a few days, when she was bored, she suggested she would do the washing up, if I liked. I let her do it. Another day she offered to baby-sit for us if we wanted to go out. I agreed with some doubts about her character; we still didn't know much about her and we had no locks on anything in our house. She also suggested she could do the ironing while listening to the children. So I set the ironing board in the kitchen and gave her a few easy things to press, like towels. We were visiting friends. I warned her about turning off the iron when she finished. She assured me by saying "Yes chodjoukh chem", "I am not a child".

Off we went, and hardly turning the corner I realised I had left a parcel I was supposed to take with me. So Krikor stopped the car to let me go back home and fetch it. I opened the door downstairs and the first thing that I sensed was a smell of burning. I ran upstairs and what did I see? Koharig had left the hot iron on the floorboard burning a hole in the wood while she was watching television.

She was startled when I shouted "What are you doing, the iron is on the floor?" She answered, "Why did you come back so early?" "Stupid girl, you were burning my house." I pulled the plug out, lifted the iron and poured water on the floor which was still smouldering. She was standing there watching me without even apologising. She said "I was only away one second, I was going to see it anyway".

She wasn't worth arguing with. I put the ironing board away. I took the parcel I had come back for and left without saying a word. My poor husband was wondering why I had taken so long. I told him. We discussed whether we should return home, and decided we would go ahead to our friends but would not stay long.

That Sunday when I came out of the church from the side door, I saw a small gathering outside the main door where a girl was crying and talking to the small crowd. I recognised her, it was Koharig. I went a few paces away and asked someone coming from there "why is she crying, what happened to her?" "Oh", said the man, "that poor girl is staying with a family and they are so mean, they make her work hard like a slave and just give her scraps of food; she is always hungry but she has no money, nowhere to go."

My first reaction was to rush to her and slap her face, then I controlled my anger, I went home instead and immediately told my husband what I witnessed. "What do we do now? Are we going to let her stay or ask her to pack her bags and get out?" He said, "That will only make things worse. She may broadcast to the world that we were so horrid, we threw her out, and even worse things that we haven't done, like abusing her, or assaulting her, and people may believe her."

I let him have his way. We pretended we knew nothing of her despicable and incriminating behaviour. During lunch I asked her if the Service was nice. She said "Didn't you come?" I said, "I didn't stay very long, I had to prepare lunch." I decided to make her ashamed of herself. I even gave her a bigger portion than ours. She devoured every scrap on her plate. Still, no thank you or anything. What kind of creature were we harbouring under our roof, was she human? Not only was she not appreciative or thankful, she was also rude, argumentative and answered back spitefully. She even spread lies and malicious gossip between us and our friends. I had to warn them when I realised what she was up to.

My husband tried to question Chalikian and discuss ways of sending her back. But he wasn't helpful. He said he didn't know her that well either. He just felt sorry for her when he found her crying in some other place. She was a clever so-and-so, crafty and manipulative.

Eventually after some months she was sent the money to go home. We certainly took a deep breath. What an experience that was! A couple of years later, one Sunday morning, our doorbell rang. I opened the door and who did I see? It was Koharig! I nearly had a heart attack, but I needn't have. She was all smiles, she said she was just back from the States staying with friends; had been to church in St. Sarkis, and thought she would call and thank us for our hospitality two years ago. She realised she behaved badly she said, when she went to America and stayed with another family everything and everybody was so different, "I couldn't even compare them with you in any way. I hadn't met such decent people like you anywhere else". She said she was very sorry she had been a nuisance and wondered how we put up with her!

I let her say all those words, occasionally trying to stop her, and thought for a moment that maybe she was trying to put a foot in the door again. On the contrary, she put her arms round me and kissed me and said she had brought me a small present. My husband and I were speechless. I asked her if she would stay for lunch, but she said she was invited somewhere else. She hugged me again and we parted on friendly terms. It was an unbelievable encounter. We had given her a lesson she couldn't forget. My husband was right. As Christ commanded us to turn the other cheek, we had done exactly that.

In his profession, conscientious as Krikor was, he often undercharged his patients, and if they were friends, or friends of friends, or clergy, student, relation or with some kind of connection, he wouldn't charge at all. NHS charges were peanuts. As he did not do any shopping at all he had no idea of how much the cost of living had gone up. I couldn't say anything, he was a proud man. As far as he was concerned we were comfortable and lacking nothing. Had I been a demanding person he might have had to change his ways. We needed few luxuries, and lived within our means. For thirty years we were married and were never apart; we were together day and night. It was like being married for 60 years without a break from each other. It was partnership in the full meaning of the word, one that never faltered. Not only was I his wife and the mother of his children, but I was also his receptionist and book keeper. It worked. We both made it work.

The lessons my husband has given me are so many. His wisdom had no bounds. Some of his friends from the American University of Beirut used to visit us on their way to or from Beirut and America. I don't think they were impressed to see our simple and unassuming lifestyle in the heart of London, because they never paid us a second visit. I never forget one of those professionals from Beirut who had just been to see another old friend, an alumnus, now in the States, the land of opportunity, who had made so good that our visitor couldn't hide his disappointment on seeing us. He must have compared our unpretentious house with that of his other friend! He said to us, with mildly disguised contempt, "Your friend X has a big villa in L.A. with a swimming pool and a garage full of the latest models".

This man wasn't my friend and I didn't want to reply even though I knew what to say. My poor darling was made very uncomfortable, especially in front of me, but managed to say a few things like, "You know, when you are working for the NHS, you are not free to charge what you want and besides, where would I put a swimming pool here? I just go across the road to my club, the pool over there is big enough for fifty. I am not complaining, nor is my wife. We have a nice family and are well known in our community. I think we are quite satisfied with our lot."

When that ostentatious man left, I said to Krikor mischievously, "You know, I think I am having second thoughts. Maybe I should have gone to America after all". For a split second, he thought I meant it, until he saw the sarcasm on my face. I gave him a hug to reassure him. There was no pretence in our life. We were not out to impress anybody. Contentment was our reward. Honest, hard work within our means. His legacy to me and his children, his nearest and dearest: No fortune, I'm afraid, but a name that is worth a million!

CHAPTER 14 DISASTER LOOMS

Krikor was a very healthy man, he had been very sportive in the past as the best footballer of the regiment and had received a medal with his name engraved on it. He was a strong swimmer at sea, and used the indoor pool of the Kensington Close Hotel opposite our home where he was a member, every morning in all weathers. He had never been ill in all his life, never even taken an aspirin for a headache.

Until the unexpected happened. He kept it secret from me for a whole year. I was suspicious of his mysterious visits to the hospital. He would dismiss my questions by saying that he was just going for a routine check-up. Even our friend and doctor, Dr. Derounian, was sworn to secrecy, and when Krikor knew that I knew, he made me swear that I wouldn't tell the children and specially, would not disrupt Michèle's education in the States.

It was Anna at first who became anxious and wrote to me from Geneva, "What's going on, how is Daddy?". However much I tried to dismiss her doubts, she guessed. At this stage we both did not know what it was that we were supposed to keep secret. Then I was told it was a prostate problem and he would be operated to fix it. Pure and simple. I didn't know what it entailed, or whether it was curable or not. He had that dreaded operation at St. Stephens Hospital in Fulham. No one would tell me about the details, whether it was successful or not. I wasn't given to consider it as a dangerous illness.

There was no one there when I visited him one day; he was all alone in the four-bedded ward, looking semi-conscious and in pain, a bag full of blood on the floor. He didn't look at me or didn't see me. I ran out calling "Nurse, nurse!". Eventually somebody heard me and followed me to his bed. I was alarmed and tearful. When I questioned her she was evasive. She just said, "Oh, it's nothing, I'll change the bag". I said, "I want to see the doctor". "I'm afraid they are all at the theatre, there is no one here at the moment" she replied. I couldn't bear her indifference and coldness. On my insistence she promised to get someone to see him as soon as possible. It broke my heart to see my poor husband left unattended, all alone, and yet he said, "Don't worry darling, they come and see me quite often. I'll be all right. You go home, don't stay here." I sat down beside him for a little while, holding his hand. He asked me if everything was all right at home, if I was managing, if I had enough money, if anyone was coming to view the house, which we'd put on the market. He just wanted to distract my attention. They brought him a cup of tea and I helped him drink slowly. He said "Please go, it'll be the rush hour soon, go!" I told him I was going to see the doctor, but he insisted that he would speak to him, and that I was not to worry... At that moment the nurse came to change his bag, and asked me to leave.

I don't know how I came home that day. I left the hospital in a daze, walking through the crowds of office workers rushing to the Underground. I followed them, passing through the gates and boarding the train like a robot. If anyone had asked me my name I am sure I wouldn't have known the answer. "Go back home" he had said. I came home. The whole house was empty, all five floors of it. Once it had been lived in, noisy, boisterous. Someone was always running up or down the stairs. We never walked, we ran. Doors slamming, telephone ringing, music, television, the girls calling each other from floor to floor, me telling them to be quiet, the doorbell ringing and a patient being admitted to the waiting room. That waiting room was now so nice and tidy, the magazines still on the centre table, not a cushion out of place, furniture nicely polished, but empty, empty ... I went up slowly to my kitchen-dining room, the hub of our house, where I would cook my family's dinner, set the table and call "come on everybody, dinner's ready!". I now stand and look around. How long since those noises stopped? How long since I cooked a meal and served, and someone would remark "that smells nice, what is it?". My cooker is nice and clean. I don't bother to use it much these days. A cup of tea would be nice. Yes, I just put the kettle on. I have plenty of time now. Nobody asking me to do anything. Everyone is away.

It is a bit scary to sleep in a big empty house all alone. You imagine things, even hear noises that can't be explained. Was that the upstairs door banging? Is there a draft coming from somewhere? I go upstairs to check all the windows and doors. Some of them don't shut properly, they rattle. Krikor always used to repair things around the house. Anything that was broken or loose. And the leaking roof! That was his main preoccupation. He often went up on it to check for cracks. That roof, supposedly re-surfaced by experts, was our black hole. We dreaded torrential rain, because it also rained indoors, on the stairs leading up to the top floor. I would put small containers for drops on the steps, and big ones for the non-stop falls. And now that the house was for sale and people would occasionally come to view it, if it was a rainy day, I would keep those containers until the very last second before anyone came, and quickly hide them so that the steps would be dry and no one would notice that our roof was leaking.

I was a master of camouflage. I knew all the likely faults that buyers would look for, and I knew exactly how to conceal them. The play acting went on for two years, but I had to lower the price a couple of times.

My priority was my husband's health. On the other hand, there were no incoming cheques but expenses hadn't stopped. I wondered sometimes how long I could go on for. There were the usual bills, rates, taxes, electricity, gas, telephone, and in the winter it was even worse. We had no central heating, but gas or electric heaters in the rooms. I had a paraffin heater in the hall that burnt day and night, and I had to fetch paraffin in gallon cans. I would put them in my shopping trolley and push them to the nearest garage in Earl's Court Road to fill them. Apart from that, I had a calor gas heater that was on all day to keep the basement dry, and I had to have the empty drum taken out and a full one put in every week which wasn't cheap. Even though the house had only one occupant now, the expenses continued all the same. I didn't realise money could melt so easily.

I tried to hide many things from Krikor. When he asked me if the boiler was working and providing hot water, I lied and said "Oh, yes, don't worry, everything is all right". I didn't tell him that I couldn't keep the fire going anymore, that the coal just wouldn't burn however much I tried.

One day I noticed in the basement that not only couldn't I get the fire going but also that the coal and the ashes were wet; there was some water coming from somewhere. That was a danger sign; it was serious trouble. By that time Krikor had been transferred to Westminster Hospital. As usual he questioned me about the boiler, he knew what a temperamental old thing it was and wondered if I could still cope.

The time had come to tell him about the wetness. He realised I hadn't been telling him the truth. He said, "Go home straight away and immediately call Krikor Altounian, he knows how to deal with it, it has to be drained or it will burst". I did exactly as he told me and our dear old friend sent his own worker. It took him a whole day to drain the boiler and connecting pipes, with long hoses carrying the water to the patio. From then on there was not even lukewarm water anymore.

My goodness! As if I didn't have enough to worry about. I managed to keep myself economically clean, I had done that kind of thing for years in the past, I was used to it. But my daughter who was here at the time needed her daily bath. Just heat dozens of kettles of water to fill half a bathtub! I don't want to think about it now, nevertheless it all comes back to me. Those black days, when anything that could go wrong, did go wrong. And I had to deal with all that by myself.

Today, as I write these lines sitting in my warm and cosy flat, where I have abundant hot water supplied without any effort on my part, it seems hard to believe. And now, in my old age, I am reasonably comfortable, and he is not here to share with me a well earned retirement, enjoying himself in leisure activities, taking up a hobby, travelling or mostly keeping me company. Solitude is my companion and I even talk to myself occasionally, or even to the walls! I never envied anybody's possessions in all my life, or good fortune in anything. I was quite satisfied with my lot and what I had was more than enough, as long as I had my husband and my children. I worked very hard to keep them all well and happy. But now that I am all alone, even though I manage and struggle along with aches and pains, as long as they don't cripple me, I cannot help feeling a tiny twinge of envy when I pass old couples in the street arm in arm, supporting each other, quite content with their lot, as long as they are together.

I know things don't last forever the way they are, and one day one of them will have to go first, but I too wanted to have my lifelong companion, my soul mate, to age with me, for us to grow old together, share everyday difficulties together, go places together, and at night, watch a film or listen to a radio programme, discuss things, enjoying each other's company.

He went much too soon, leaving me to carry on alone. I have been a widow for 22 years now. It was very hard at first. Thanks to my wonderful friends and colleagues who supported me, I kept sane and busy.

Many of my good friends are no longer with us. My dearest Jeanette, who was the wife of the jeweller, Sdepan Aydinian, died a long time ago; fortunately her sister Mimi took her place in my affections, and what a friend she has been, and all the others, like the very lovely Shaké and loyal and selfless Hayguhi who was always running to help others until she had that terrible stroke. Those two are irreplaceable. Then a few more, the luckless Sirvart, the poor thing who suffered so much, and Alice Keshishian, Siran Shamlian, and the incomparable Sandrunys who were my rock during my husband's last days and afterwards. Just next door to us Berdj Sandruny used to be the resident secretary of the Armenian House and his wife Beatrice was in our Ladies Committee. What fantastic people they were. The fact that I was kept busy with such a supportive team allowed me to exist in a pretence of resignation.

After all those years I didn't have to stir up painful memories. They were truly buried for a long time when so much has happened since. Maybe I was wrong to start writing this saga, which, instead of getting shorter heading towards the end seems unstoppable now. Many episodes have surfaced, slipping through the net of oblivion. It is like a whirlwind treasure hunt, I am zigzagging backwards and forwards through the past. I cannot cut the thread mid course in case I lose the continuity. One minute I am with my school children and then the next, at the hospital with my dying husband. Why did I start doing this impossible task? Will anybody bother to read it? Is it interesting enough or a boring story?

During his illness at the hospital, I was going to and fro, trying to be in both places. I had to check with estate agents, arrange viewing times with prospective buyers and hope against hope that when they said "We will let you know" they meant it. I had umpteen visitors of all nationalities. They liked the house for its location, but because it was not in very good condition they were put off. In the meantime, whenever my husband had a reprieve and was sent home, we went to see many properties ourselves. Sometimes he would be very hopeful and believe that we could still be together for a while, and fancy having a little bijou house with a small manageable garden in a quiet residential area. We used to sift through agents' ads to find such an ideal cottage and build our dreams, daydreams, that were not to materialise. Even if we had found a desirable residence we couldn't have moved until our own house was sold. I did not know then how much time we had left and thought it may be a couple more years.

But it wasn't to be. It was a no-win situation, and Krikor realised it before I did. One day, when he had been home on remission, he called me to come and sit by him on the sofa. He cleared his throat before saying what was to come.

"You know darling, we have to talk seriously." I sat down very close to him, next to his emaciated frame. Even his voice was thin and shaky, though that could have been by emotion. I squeezed his hand to give him heart. His voice was calm and hesitant.

"Anahid, it's no use, let's not kid ourselves anymore, no more pretending, it won't happen." I swallowed very hard not to cry. I was holding my breath. He paused for courage. "From now on we don't have to look for a house with a garden ... no need ... no need. Let's be practical. You can't manage it all by yourself."

Another pause. I didn't dare to look at his face. I wanted to burst.

"No house ... no garden. It will be too much for you. Things go wrong in a house, roof, gutters, heating. You can't deal with builders and plumbers. They'll make your life hell. Listen, I think you should get yourself a small flat, a nice little place, where things are done for you. It will be easier."

He couldn't say any more, he had said enough and even too much. His voice was going and I couldn't bear it any longer. We put our heads together and cried silently, tears flowing, our wet faces close together, until my sobbing started. I was crying uncontrollably. He was the first to stop and collect himself ... I got up to reach for the Kleenex box. He kept saying, "Come, come, let's be realistic. It has to happen one day. No one is immortal." I passed him a tissue and another, we both finished the box. Months of frustration and repressed feelings and pretence had gone out of the window. He just wanted to prepare me for the worst. He was my best friend and his concern for me went even beyond his grave.

We sat silently for a while. He whispered now with pauses now and then. "I know it will be hard at first but the girls will be there, you'll manage, you'll manage. You still have a long life ahead of you. You are only just sixty. I hate to think that you may be lonely. I would be happier if I knew you had someone to take care of you, I really would, someone kind and sensible, unselfish."

I stopped him there. "What are you talking about, what do you mean? You are not going anywhere yet, and I don't want to think that far ahead, and I hate what you are suggesting!" And cried some more. He held my hand. "I mean it, I wish you could meet a good kind person to look after you, keep you company." I got angry, "Don't be silly, don't say things like that, I can't bear it, it's awful."

Oh! What a day it was. Now that I write those lines, rather reluctantly, those utterly private moments that so far I have not told anyone, not a soul, I still think that maybe, at the last minute, if this book ever gets to be printed I may yet omit them. That episode was so intimate and so tender and heartbreaking that I cannot live through the memory without a resurgence of tears, and write these lines through clouded eyes.

22 years have since passed and never was I slightly tempted even to think of another partner, nor consider a part-time companion as a substitute. The thought alone is so repugnant to me. Surprisingly, some years later, when I had organised my life and was sure of my new status as a confirmed widow, satisfied with my lot, I had a proposal from an honourable and professional gentleman for companionship for outside activities, like theatre outings, travelling abroad, on the basis of a purely platonic friendship. I was dismayed, as I had never encouraged anybody towards that kind of rapprochement. Without sounding rude, I thanked him and flatly refused and asked him not to try to persuade me again. The answer would always be NO.

There isn't a day that I don't speak to Krikor. His almost life-size photographic portrait in a gold frame is hanging in my bedroom opposite my bed. It is the last thing I see at night and the first thing in the morning. In my troubled days when I have a problem, he is the first one I open my heart to and seek inspiration from. As far as I am concerned I am still married to him, the most honest, righteous, infuriatingly stubborn and upright man I have ever come across. He was my soul mate, my best friend, my husband, and the one who guided me through uncertain times.

I still believe that Providence had a lot to do with my life, stopped me going to America, that all the time my fate was determined. I might have been richer there and might have led a glamorous life, but no thanks, I have no regrets. I have had a full and meaningful life, a wonderful and contented existence.

If only Krikor hadn't suffered so much. Every time he was sent home we were hoping it would be a long while before he needed to go back again. He did not wish to receive visitors at home, he'd had a few of those at hospital, like the Sandrounys and Bessak Serpazan, Mr. Moutafian, Dr. Derounian, Nerses Serpazan, Mr. Artan, and I was always there with them as he didn't like making conversation, I tried to cut those visits short. The same happened at home; he wanted to rest quietly with me alone, spend as much quality time together as possible. If anyone called to ask would it be all right to come and see him, I somehow tried to put him off very politely, "maybe another time, I'll let you know".

In August 1980, he was sent home again. This time it wasn't just a reprieve; it was to be his last visit, but I didn't know it then. With the help of Mrs. Childs, our dear old and faithful home help, I prepared a bed for him in the dining room on the first floor next to our living room. Those two rooms had an inter-communicating door that I kept open; when he slept in his new bed at night I would make myself comfortable on the sofa so that I could keep an eye on him all the time. For those two weeks I never let him out of my sight. I stopped taking my sleeping pill to be alert at all times. As he was bedridden, two nurses would come every morning to give him a wash and change, and the rest of the time I had to look after him, feed him, mainly liquids, make him comfortable, and give him his medication at various times. A chart was stuck on the wallpaper next to his bed which I consulted every hour to see when the next pill was due.

I gave him mostly soups or very soft mashed up food as he had difficulty swallowing. The Sister at the hospital used to make an egg nog specially for him, which was a very nourishing and palatable drink. I decided to make that for him too, a mixture of beaten egg with milk and brandy. He had no appetite and I had to coax him to eat or drink.

The only visitors he could manage were the Sandrunys, who lived next door in the Armenian House and had become close friends as a result of his illness. They would always pass him greetings from his colleagues. His beloved Armenian House was far away from his thoughts now; not because he did not care, but because he was no use to it anymore. He was no use to anybody. He was helpless and he realised that with pain in his heart. No one needed him now. But I did, I wanted to keep him alive as long as possible. I hated to see that he was slipping away gradually from my grasp. On his last visit, Archbishop Bessak Toumayan gave him the last rites and prayed softly and movingly. When I took him downstairs to see him out, he said "Anahid, may God give you courage". He knew what was to follow soon.

It was the last Thursday, 14th of August 1980, we both had a disturbing night. He was uncomfortable, I was up near his bed, he was sleeping on and off at short stretches. I wasn't. I didn't want to in case I missed something. And I was tired, and weary and restless at the same time. I spoke to him in whispers, in very soft voices, not knowing whether he was awake or not. His eyes were half open and so was his mouth. He couldn't breathe properly. I gave him his medication but wasn't sure whether it was going down or not. I had put my chair next to his bed waiting for him to say something. Sometimes his lips would move and I could tell he was thirsty and gave him some water through a straw.

I tried to read and sometimes would be dozing for a few minutes and wake up startled. He would be watching me through his half-open eyes. I wonder what he thought, or felt. He must have realised he had not got long to go. But I was always hoping that as long as I was there for him day and night no one could take him away from me. But that was not living.

CHAPTER 15 MY GREAT LOSS

That night the telephone rang. It was my son-in-law calling from the hospital where Sonia had gone to have her second child. He said: "Good news, we've got a baby boy!" I screamed with happiness and ran inside to tell him "Darling, Sonia had a baby boy!" He smiled or tried to, his lips moved a little bit and his eyes shone for a split second. He nodded slightly, to say he understood. I tried to cheer him up by making plans aloud for Sonia to bring the baby as soon as she was out of hospital and we would kiss and cuddle him. And I wondered what they would call him. I was saying all sorts of things whether they would make sense or not, to keep him awake and see if I could get a word from him. He was just listening to whatever I was saying with a faint smile. I thought that's what it was, and gradually he went to sleep.

That night I gave Anna a call in Geneva. I gave her the latest news that Sonia's baby boy was born. She gave a joyous shriek. She was happy at last to get some good news for a change. She then asked about Daddy. "Mummy shall I come?" I said, "Darling, I don't know how much time we have got. Probably a week or less, I really don't know."

I was careful to shut the door and whisper those words. He was deep in sleep anyway. I spent the rest of the night praying and occasionally dropping off. I didn't even bother to change into my night clothes. In the morning when the nurses came they could hardly move him. They came to see me in the kitchen where I was making them a cup of tea. "I think you should call the doctor," said the senior nurse. "He should go to hospital."

The doctor came and called the ambulance straight away. I got his things ready and told Mrs. Sandruny to tell Anna if she called.

She stayed in our house while Mr. Sandruny accompanied me in the ambulance going to the hospital. They managed to find him a bed in a crowded ward. I stayed with him in the ward but our friend decided he had to get back. He was very moved by what was happening to us.

Not much later Anna arrived. She had cancelled a contract and had taken the first available flight from Geneva to be with me, she got my message, and took a taxi to the hospital. After staying with him for a while the nurse said that there was no point in waiting much longer, soon it would be supper-time and we should go. It was getting late and there was nothing we could have done, probably we were in the way. His eyes shone ever so slightly seeing Anna but he couldn't say a thing. We both kissed him good night and promised to be there early next morning.

Anna was the only one of his children to be able to see him in hospital for the last time. We came home hardly able to speak together. We were both thinking the same thing.

His bed was empty. I left it as it was. I couldn't touch it. I went up to my own bed where I hadn't slept for two weeks. As soon as I woke up in the morning, I came down to be by the phone. We didn't have one upstairs. Anna joined me. We were both on edge, we knew that if there was a call it wouldn't be good news.

On the 16th of August 1980, at 7.30 in the morning, we had the dreaded news. Anna took the call. She would have to go to the hospital and receive the relevant official papers needed for the death certificate. She left immediately to get the documents done. I don't know what I would have done without her. I couldn't even think straight. Now, what should we do next? I just wanted to be left alone and remember exactly what had happened the last few days so that I would never forget for the rest of my life. I visualised the way he looked lying in his deathbed at home, all his medicines lined up on the trolley, bottles and pills and the chart showing the times to be taken, his glass of water still half full, his specs, his slippers that he hadn't worn recently. Why didn't I take them to hospital this time? Did I know he wouldn't need them anymore? His unmade bed I wouldn't dare make or unmake. I left it as it was for a few days. There was a storm in my head. Too much past and present mingled, I couldn't separate in my mind.

Anna came back with the necessary papers, "Krikor Gorgodian deceased". Simple. I just said to her, "What do we do now?" How was I going to organise the funeral service, etc? Anna thought we should immediately tell the Sandrunys and Serpazan to organise everything. I was helpless. Funeral, Church, cemetery, reception. If I could, I would forget about all that and have time for myself to mourn quietly and re-live the last moments together and still feel his presence.

I wasn't allowed to waste time. There were things to do. Bessak Serpazan came shortly with the Sandrunys to discuss the arrangements. I wanted them to do everything necessary and just let me know what they had decided. Serpazan was in charge here. I cannot remember now who gave it to him, but he produced an envelope left by Krikor for me, which he opened there and then. Those were his last wishes and advice to me and the children, written in Armenian, by his own hand. He did not want to be buried. He wished to be cremated and his ashes to be scattered in the sea. Also, telling me, how much he loved me and his daughters and telling them to love, honour and respect their mother.

May God bless their souls, Serpazan's and the Sandrunys'. The Church funeral service, the cremation at Golders Green and the limousines were all to be organised by Kenyons, Funeral

Directors, the reception afterwards in the Armenian House by the Ladies Committee under the direction of Mrs. Sandruny and my friend Vehanoush Gulvanessian. I didn't have to do anything. I was given a couple of valiums by my doctor and supported by my children, I managed to follow the service like a robot and the coffin to the cemetery through half-open eyes.

They told me that St. Peter's church was absolutely packed. The only notice we placed was in the Daily Telegraph obituary column, announcing his death and the time and date of the funeral service. Additionally, a wish that, in lieu of flowers, donations for an educational grant in Dr. Gorgodian's name be sent to the Armenian House. About £1,500 was raised, which, later on, I would share out to a few suitable applicants on interviewing them. Despite our wish there were also lots of flowers.

The Ladies Committee did me proud and I was grateful for the lavish reception they had organised to a full capacity of mourners who had gathered at the A. H. for refreshments. Sonia managed to leave the hospital in time to come to her father's funeral. The baby was at home with a friend.

What an unforgettable day that was. I don't know how I managed to attend all those ceremonies half existing, see his coffin go behind that final curtain and disappear. I kept myself respectfully standing, leaning and supported on either side, and listened to that magnificent oration that Mr. Yessayan gave in the Chapel. I didn't understand everything, I didn't hear properly, my head was in clouds, but the text was given to me later. And also Serpazan's address at the Church, so moving and sincere.

The next few days after the funeral I didn't want to see or speak to anyone. I became a recluse. There was a morbid silence in the house. The girls put the television on when I was not in the living room. I think they were just watching the news or a documentary. I don't think they were in the mood for anything else. Sonia wanted to take her new baby home and Anna had to go back to Geneva. At home the cupboard was bare, no serious shopping had been done for some time, and I had to think of Michèle.

The tears I shed those days could fill a small pond. My eyes were sore and my face was distorted. I put my sunglasses on, I wanted to hide behind them. Who cares? I didn't wish to receive any visitors. There was no need. Those who could come to the funeral did. Many patients sent letters or cards. Anna was in charge of responding to all donors to the Educational Grant, and those who sent flowers. The dozens of beautiful cards and messages written with so much feeling and admiration for their wonderful dentist who had taken such good care of their teeth: although I appreciated people's sympathy, I regret I was in no state to respond. I have still kept a big batch of condolence and sympathy cards.

I knew all Krikor's patients personally, they had been coming to him for many years from even far away places: when they moved house they still kept coming to him travelling some distances. They didn't trust anybody else. He was not just a good dentist, he was a very honest, patient and kind man. And they were very appreciative of him. I regret to say, some of his Armenian patients used to take advantage of his kindness by turning up unexpectedly at unsuitable hours, sometimes late at night or on Sundays after the church service while passing our door on their way to the Armenian House. They would ring the bell just as we were sitting at the table to have our lunch. "Aman (Oh) doctor, while I am here, it would be nice if you would see this bad tooth of mine, it saves me making this journey again." It was convenient for them but I resented the fact that they were taking his kindness for granted. He knew it too, but always obliged without complaining. There would be a war of words but I always let him have the last word. I hated those confrontations all because of other people's selfishness. He was too good and it hurt me to see him being taken for a ride. It wasn't weakness on his part, never complaining, always excusing others, whereas I would wage war against such people who were inconsiderate to say the least.

Even in later years when he was getting weaker by the day, dignified as he was, he wished to keep his good name. He was very protective of his reputation, the name "Gorgodian" should never be tarnished, and we were all conscious of that obligation.

According to his last wishes Krikor was cremated in Golders Green, but on my own initiative I had arranged for a rose tree to be planted on half of his ashes that I kept paying for and visiting at first weekly, then monthly, until it became impossible for me to go there alone, and needed someone to take me: it was too far away. It would be some weeks before I could visit my rose bush with the inscription "We'll meet again" and his name and date of death. It was such a beautiful and peaceful place, like the gardens of Eden; trees, shrubs and colourful flowers. No one about to disturb you and your thoughts. A place for contemplation! In later years I used to be nervous being alone in that quiet stillness. The silence was deafening, you heard nothing, and if there was a stir in the air, it scared me so much imagining all those ghosts floating around me, and without even looking behind I used to walk as fast as I could to find the path leading me out. Finally, I resolved never to go there alone again. I felt I was being watched and I could imagine hearing whispers. I made a final payment and asked the office if I could buy my rose bush that was planted on his ashes. They refused. I had been visiting it for twenty years. I said my final goodbyes leaving the bush behind.

Soon after the cremation 22 years ago, and according to his wishes I had half of his ashes put in a casket, which Michèle and I took on the ferry to the Isle of Wight and halfway there we dropped the casket in the sea with our prayers. That was his wish and it was done. May he rest in peace. No grave to visit, but as I promised, "We'll meet again".

I am sure my feelings of resentment, desolation and despair were also felt by many a widow and widower who were devastated when their beloved spouse passed away. I know I was not the only one in this situation but I can only speak for myself and those who have been in a similar circumstance will understand and sympathise with the acuteness and bitterness of my emotions. Some much younger than I was, or even at my age then, might have made a brave new attempt to find companionship for a second time. I don't blame them. Even my husband suggested that I should seek "a good kind man to take care of me". But is that enough? To be taken care of? I couldn't love another man and it wouldn't be fair on that person to be just a puppet, have responsibilities but no expectations. *No, no one can replace him.*

CHAPTER 16 COMMUNITY AFFAIRS

I felt alone at first, but my friends, colleagues, associates, all the organisations I worked for and my commitments to those various committees, the umpteen meetings I attended, Church Council, Cultural, AGBU and their Ladies, Hayasdan Fund, and most of all the Armenian House Trustees and the Ladies Committee, came to fill the vacuum in my life. I threw myself wholeheartedly into their activities, organising, chairing, taking down minutes and writing letters, speech making and was never bored or doing nothing. In fact, if anything, I overdid it. I also took up my correspondence with the Jamanak Newspaper once more, my column entitled "Londonian Namagani" (London Newsletter), was welcome back over there, in Istanbul. On popular demand I started organising my successful daytrips which became an annual institution. All these activities didn't leave much time for wallowing in self-pity during the day. It was the nights that I dreaded, when I would be physically exhausted as well.

Apart from all that, I also had my family, daughters and grandchildren, to hold together, and visiting relatives and friends from abroad; I made myself available to them all.

For the daytrips, I hired huge 57-seater coaches that were always filled to capacity. I used two pick up points, A.H. in Kensington and Chiswick Town Hall. We visited most of the South Coast seaside towns, some more than once, from Bournemouth down to the Kent coast, the Isle of Wight a few times. All the cathedrals, stately homes, royal palaces, museums, gardens and parks, Stratford-on-Avon (Shakespeare's home town) three times, Alton Towers, Greenwich by river-boat three times, Stonehenge, Bath and Salisbury Cathedral all in one day, the Silk Factory and Leeds Castle in one day, Cadbury's chocolate factory, wine-tasting at Denby's vineyard twice, across the Channel by ferry twice to Boulogne and once to Calais, Althorpe House four times, Sandringham House and many many more. And in all the cathedrals we visited, including St. Paul's, we sang the Lord's Prayer in Armenian before the altar, after first asking permission, of course. We held two fashion shows at the Armenian House. I conducted an interview with Princess Helena Moutafian, in front of an invited audience. We even visited the Regents Park Mosque which scandalised Nerses Serpazan so much so that he devoted one Sunday's sermon entirely to that "outrageous act" committed under my guidance: "instead of visiting a cathedral, our ladies go to a mosque!" When he was in power here in London, I had confronted him privately regarding his unjust and unfair treatment towards Bessak Serpazan. I suspect he never forgot my disregard for his authority.

Ever since our Embassy was established in London, the Ladies Committee of the Armenian House has helped it to host and organise their stand at the International Charity Fair that takes place every year in mid-May at the Kensington Town Hall. We also help them in any way we can for their occasional receptions. The Ladies' main duties lie in organising fund raising events for the A.H. and help with the refurbishment of the House. We also have monthly social gatherings for all Armenian women in a cordial atmosphere with coffee and pastries. This is a standing invitation and free of charge that has been going on for over thirty years.

One of the most unforgettable characters to hold a special place of respect in my memory is the late Mr. Haroutune Moutafian with whom I worked for many years under his chairmanship, both in the Armenian House Trustees and the executive of AGBU (Armenian General Benevolent Union). He was very knowledgeable in constitutional affairs of both these organisations. He was a first class chairman, authoritative as well as friendly. He ran his meetings very efficiently and had a good rapport with his colleagues. He was an excellent host opening his grand house for special receptions during the visit of high ranking guests like the Catholicos and the Life President of the AGBU, Mr. Alex Manougian and his wife Marie, and later on his daughter Louise. Princess Helena Moutafian was the hostess with the mostest, gracious, welcoming and generous.

Another colleague I respected very much in the AGBU was our secretary, Mr. Garbis Yessayan. His mastery of our language, his most excellent Armenian, has influenced me to better myself in taking down the minutes of the AGBU meetings for many years with him at the helm. His speeches are unique in their literary context, unfortunately, sometimes, well above the ordinary folks' appreciation. He is an excellent orator and I enjoy listening to him whenever I am in his audience. He is also an expert on constitutional affairs and has written the Tekeyan Cultural Association's constitution. I am sure I am not the only one admiring him as he has a great many ex-students from Jerusalem and Cyprus who owe him gratitude from their schooldays. He and his wife, Anahid, are among my friends.

*   *   *   *

When the unforgettable earthquake shook our Country as well as our beings in 1988, the whole community became one in determination to help our devastated people. Aid Armenia was born and took offices in the Armenian House, the most available and convenient place. A committee was elected and volunteers offered their services selflessly. Before the Aid Armenia's occupation of the ground floor, our Ladies Committee set to work there organising a collection centre for warm clothing, blankets and anything useful to be sent to Armenia.

We had a lot of help from everybody who came to give us a hand. The response from donors was overwhelming: even non-Armenians, tourists, the Hotel opposite sending us brand new blankets; the generosity of schools, local organisations and the British people at large was quite unforgettable.

The entrance door of the A.H. was left open, some Armenian youth were standing at the door to receive financial donations. A woman came with a large jar full of pound coins. She said "I have been collecting it all this year, it is my holiday money. I don't want it any more, you need it more than I do." I had tears in my eyes.

For a whole week, the entire ground floor of the A.H., and the basement and the stairs going up and down, were impassable. We were tidying, classifying, filling the extra large polythene bags, tying them up securely and make them ready to be taken away in lorries to the Airport. The whole of the community was at work, giving, collecting, carrying, assembling, in other centres as well. Every day my colleagues and I were on our feet from morning till dark, non stop, tired and dirty and yet with a sense of fulfilment for being of some service at this immeasurable catastrophe that hit our nation. It is unforgettable. It was like a military operation, here in England and Diaspora Armenians reaching out to the Mother Country in the face of that dreadful calamity.

I hope we won't need another disaster to bring this community together again. It breaks my heart to see our people tear each other to pieces. We have but one enemy to fight, not brother against brother. There will be no cause for fighting if we fight with each other. This is very sad; even political parties are feuding among themselves. Obviously someone has to give in. Please, pull yourselves together, otherwise we are going to lose the little Hairenik we have got left.

I have some very nice friends who belong to this or that side, they are very dear to me, but I wish they realised how much harm extreme views can cause to our National Unity. The Armenian House is probably the only establishment we have that has no party politics - and that is one of the reasons why we value it so much. It is able to remain independent, and provide a base to our Embassy and even to our Church.

*   *   *   *

I do not suppose anybody under the age of 40 will remember our first National Church, the All Saints Church, in St. Johns Wood, North London. Unfortunately, it was only in our possession for ten years. It was bright and spacious with its own car-park on its own grounds, very conveniently situated for the residents of North London. My daughter, Sonia, was married there as well as many other couples, who, I am sure, will remember that important episode in their lives, and maybe - like me - regret the missed opportunity of acquiring it for good.

So far, I have tried to avoid mentioning painful events that caused a big rift in our community, as well as the creation of our first National Church, the sacking of Archbishop Bessak Toumayan and the hostility to which he was subjected, the conflict created between his sympathisers and the opposers, and the irregularities in the elections. That was an unhappy time for our community, and sadly, even the Catholicos became involved and couldn't remain unbiased. It may be past history now, but unforgettable all the same, the humiliation and public down-grading of a high-ranking and well-loved Archbishop which not only damaged his standing but his health as well. There will never be another one like him.

I am not a historian, and my intention is not to deviate from the purpose of this book which is entirely dedicated to the personal memories and thoughts in my life first as an "unintentional immigrant" and my subsequent existence, struggles and finally settling down and building my nest in London. My family is the most important thing in my life. I also want to devote any surplus time and energy I have available to the welfare of the Armenian House.

I am among friends in the A.H. Trustees, like Haig Abadjian, our Chairman: his family were the most generous donors when purchasing the A.H. in 1961, and we have known each other for decades. And, of course, Krikor Vartoukian, the Vice-Chairman, an old friend too and one of the most active supporters of Hai Doon.

Then there are all the others: Missak Kalindjian, who was one of the pioneers, Garo Garabedian, Sdepan Ovannessof, Hratch Tokatlian, Haro Bedelian, our very competent secretary, Dr. Anoush Major, and myself - a very compact and dedicated team. To those nine will be added the Chairman and the Vice-Chairman of the newly elected Church Council, as ex-officio members.

The Ladies Committee, with old and new friends, are Araxi Heghoyan, Peggy Shishmanian, Mimi Bacon, Ojik Brose, Angèle Arevian, Yvonne Torikian, Nellie Hovsepian, Manushag Dickranian, Arevig Gazchian, Alice Garabedian, Diana Mamigonian ... sadly Rosie Gregory is housebound and can no longer join us.

I have also been happy to work with many male colleagues on various committees: Paul Gulbenkian, Barkev Kassardjian, The Rev. Vrej Nersesian, Garo Chakmakdjian, Armenag Topalian, David Messerlian, Dr. Zoulikian, Mack Pachaian, Hayasdan Vartanian, Koko Tchelbakian, Armand Keshishian, Haig Tahta, Dr. Derounian, Zareh Jerejian, Raffi Sarkissian, and those departed: Hagop Palamoudian, Manuel Keushgerian, Haig Artan, Haroutune Aivazian, Garo Krikorian and Lucas Gregory.

The Armenian House has had four resident secretaries since its inception in 1962. Mr. Hagop Gurunlian came from Greece and was the first one to hold the post, which he did for about eight years. He was followed by Mr. Zohrab Shamlian. Then, Mr. and Mrs. Berdge Sandruny, a mature and well-respected couple, who came from Cyprus and stayed until 1980 when they wished to retire. Following them, Mr. and Mrs. Dédéyan from Paris, recommended to Archbishop Toumayan by the Primate in Paris, took up the post until 1989, just after the earthquake. They were the last resident wardens. Following them, Mrs. Simolak was chosen from a list of candidates and has been running and maintaining the Armenian House in good order since then. She is adaptable, and has made herself indispensable.

After the independence of Armenia was declared, the first Armenian Embassy in London opened its offices in the Armenian House. Our Country's first ambassador, Armen Sarkissian and his wife Nouné were very appreciative of our hospitality, and a mutual co-operation and co-existence was created in the House. The Ladies Committee were always available to organise any receptions for them in the A.H. and, most importantly, to represent our Embassy at the Annual International Charity Fair at the Town Hall during the month of May.

It is a pity that I never had the courage to go to Armenia, despite my longing. I do not trust myself to be able to put up with all the hassle of long-distance travel. Due to post-operative disability resulting from my hip replacement in 1998, I am off-balance without a walking stick and a helping hand. Moreover, I suffer from food intolerance: my allergies and digestive problems combined make me a hopeless guest wherever I happen to be. I wish I were more adaptable, with strong limbs and a healthier stomach. The desire to go is as keen as ever, but I am still hesitant. So I just content myself with an unattainable dream of a pilgrimage to the Mother Country.

I love getting encouraging news from Armenia, I love our culture and our music. I love my Church and our traditions, our Badarak, our divine church music, which I find so moving, so exalting. These days, when I cannot go to Church as often as I wish to, for spiritual uplifting I immerse myself in our heavenly music on tapes and records, close my eyes, and just imagine myself to be there, in God's house.

We are a talented race, clever, intelligent, hard-working, and what do we do with all the gifts that God has given us? In a competitive world, it is difficult to shine. We want to be proud of our achievements. Whenever there is an Armenian success story, we want to hero-worship. The Aznavours and the Aghassis of this world fill us with pride, no matter that sometimes these are only part-Armenian or even, unfortunately, deny their roots, like Kasparov. But Cher has always acknowledged her Armenian origin. Then there are always newcomers, who make waves in sports, music and the arts. And multi-millionaire philanthropists who spread the benefits of their riches to humanitarian causes, like Alex Manougian and Kirk Kirkorian.

We are proud of our famous composers, like Khachadourian, and our talented musicians like Haroutune Bedelian and Levon Chilingirian, and especially their uncle, the late, well-known Manoug Parikian. And I am sure there are many more in other parts of the world that I do not know or do not remember right now. And there is a hoard of them in Armenia. Our little country is bursting with talent, but devoid of opportunity. In whatever field, we want to show the world we mean to stand and be counted. We want to have a foothold in the limelight, to hold our heads high. We have no big brother to depend on, so we have to promote ourselves and each other.

I remember one of my mother's patriotic songs that went "Voch yeghpark voch, Odarneren chiga houys". (No, brothers, no, there's no hope from strangers.) That is very true. We must have learnt our lesson by now, therefore we should form a non-partisan alliance, "tount azkayin", wipe out all hatred from our hearts, and co-operate with each other. We could then become a force to be reckoned with. If our Diaspora gets stronger, we can have greater influence on Armenia's internal affairs.

*   *   *   *

In my early thirties, when I was still an unknown, just the young wife of Dr. Gorgodian, Mrs. Benlian, the Chairman of the Community Council's Ladies Committee, asked me to join them. When I received her letter of invitation, I had no idea what joining entailed. I had never done any committee work, and all the other ladies there were so much more mature and experienced. What could I do to help them? But she was such a pleasant and gracious lady, that I could not refuse.

Every year, they organised the New Year Ball, and the children's Christmas Party. I was asked to present a 'tableau vivant' about Baby Jesus in the manger with a few children singing carols. In those days, I didn't know any carols, so after managing to find a small group of children, I thought of teaching them to sing a Nativity Hymn in Armenian, "Khorurt medz yev skantchely" (Great and wonderful mystery) which would be just right for the occasion. Foolishly, I didn't realise that none of those boys spoke Armenian, nor had even heard any carols. How naive can you be? They used to come to my house to learn the lines and practice. After a couple of sessions, I nearly gave up.

It was the hardest thing I had ever undertaken. But there was no time to change, in a few days it would be our Christmas. The 6th of January arrived. I arranged a kind of manger in a corner of the hall, a doll for baby Jesus wrapped in swaddling clothes, a pretty girl dressed suitably as the Virgin Mary, and those boys wearing our Church Choir boys' garments as Joseph and the shepherds. The picture looked quite realistic until it was time to sing. I took a deep breath and, turning my back to the audience, I joined in the singing trying to match their voices, and we managed to accomplish our most difficult and ambitious production. The children were applauded by their proud parents, while I hid myself in a corner. I could have died!

After that unexpected success, Mrs. Benlian used to ask me to take part in their cultural programmes, reciting poetry and acting in short plays. Fortunately, I still remembered a few poems from school days. I also joined the Choir that Krikor Mandossian was conducting. Until the influx of Armenians from Cyprus and the Near East, I was their star performer, but I secretly considered myself to be the 'one-eyed woman in the kingdom of the blind'!

The community then was very small in number, and it was easy to shine.

Also in 1952, during our New Year dance, Mrs. Benlian got up to deliver her welcoming speech as usual, and I congratulated her, saying how impressive it was. She said to me, "Anahid, aghchiges (my dear), one day you are going to do these things!" At the time, I just took it as a compliment; I never dreamt I could or would have the opportunity to get that far. I wonder, how did she know? Was it a prediction or a wish? In any case, it came true. One day, I too had to make a speech and I have not stopped since.

That episode is my earliest memory of my involvement in the life of this community. Since that time I worked on several committees, made many friends and had a very rich and interesting life: initially as wife and mother, then grandmother, and now great grandmother. Since I came to England I lived in two different YWCA hostels, first in Manchester then in London for three years, spent my married life first in a rented flat, then in my own home in Cheniston Gardens, and lastly, as a widow, moved to my present address, a comfortable small flat in Kensington.

The famous and not so famous have all sat on my husband's chair, well known artists, writers, diplomats, archbishops and even a patriarch. That was the late Catholicos Karekin whom I met for the last time a couple of years ago, at a reception given in his honour at Gulbenkian Hall. I went to kiss his hand and he talked to me about my husband with fond memories. I asked him jokingly, "Has he hurt you too, Vehapar?". and he replied, "Voch aghchiges, tarmanets". (No, my daughter, he treated me.) A nice way of putting it.

Manoug Parikian, our famous violinist, was a regular patient, and every time he came he would also bring his precious violin and keep it by him in the surgery. He said to me "It follows me everywhere". When he heard that my husband had retired, one day I opened the door to him and there he was trying to lift a heavy crate full of choice drinks. He just put them down inside the door and said "It is the least I can do to show my appreciation to my beloved friend of 30 years for taking such good care of my teeth". He left and went into his car. God bless both their souls.

If I start counting all the people we were friendly or associated with, I am bound to forget some important ones, or be accused of name dropping. To counteract that assumption I will recount a true incident.

One day, returning from my daily shopping, I opened the front door to enter the house and the first thing that hit me in the face was a disgusting smell which was emanating from the surgery. Nervously I pushed the door slightly to peep inside. There was an unrecognisable creature sitting in his chair, I could only see the back of a grotesque thing like a scarecrow. I shut it firmly and holding my breath ran upstairs. When, later on, I heard the front door opening and closing, I ran down, still holding my nose, to find out who it had been. It was a tramp, Krikor told me, while disinfecting everything that had come into contact with him. He had said that he was in pain and that no other dentist would see him. I don't know how Krikor managed to bend over him without a mask for half an hour to pull his tooth out, and comfort him too. That's the kind of man my husband was!

Had I been the one opening the door to him, I would probably have shut it in his face again, to that dirty, revolting, smelly, unkempt creature. And that is exactly what others had done until he came to call on us. I do not know what Krikor's first reaction had been: disgust, I imagine. He must also have had a moment of indecision as to whether he should allow him in, and then, caution, a furtive glance around in case anyone should see this filthy person entering our house and being treated with his instruments. Krikor admitted hesitating at first, but "the man was in pain and had a tear in his eye" and he couldn't turn him away. To my husband he was just one of God's creatures and needed help. Once the vagrant was properly treated and out of the way, he set out to clean and sterilise everything, and I aired and sprayed the place to get rid of all traces of the stench. I wouldn't be at all surprised if Krikor had also put some money in his hand. People who have suffered pain, rejection, poverty have something in common, an unwritten rule that creates empathy with others in similar circumstances. Krikor knew what that creature was going through, he would never have forgiven himself if he had sent him away. His compassion was boundless.

One day I remarked thoughtlessly, that immigrants were abusing the welfare system. He rebuked me. "Some of these people have every right to be here, they fought in the War for this country, they come from the Commonwealth. I know them well, I lived with them in India and Burma."

This shows that there is a lot of ignorance and prejudice and not enough goodwill even in the best of us. Who owes what to whom? Who is ruler and who is independent? We have to accept what historians tell us, as most of us haven't witnessed the atrocities of the past. Sometimes it is the elders telling the young their tales of hardship. We believe them, but where is the evidence that cynics want?

Volumes have been written about the Jewish holocaust; there is always a reference either in the papers or on radio and television, let alone on old films. Repetition of the past echoes until we cannot take any more. I do not for one moment wish to suggest that it is not true. But enough is enough. No one speaks of our own genocide. When it comes to our case no one wants to know, they dismiss it as past history, "it happened so long ago, forget it!" Besides, we haven't got a big brother. And not only that, worst of all, we have no solidarity. Jews from all over the world went to Israel to help build their newly acquired country with their bare hands. Whereas, our people are leaving Armenia by the thousands for a better life elsewhere. When I commented on this issue to a former Armenian citizen, she said to me, "if you care so much, then you go and live there".

As a nation we have many good qualities and yet we don't have "savoir-faire", rather like a rough diamond in need of polishing. At times, it seems to me we are burdened with sadness, and lack humour. Also, we can be too self-conscious, perhaps, with an inferiority complex?

For us life is very serious. We need loosening up. When I first came to England in 1946, I thought this was the dullest country besides having the dullest food. It didn't take me long to realise that I was wrong. I have learnt many things since then. What took me longer to learn was the British sense of humour. When Gracie Fields, their beloved Lancashire born singer, used to sing in peculiar voices I could not appreciate people's enjoyment. "Why doesn't she sing properly?" I asked. She could, if she wanted to. If you haven't heard Gracie's "funny" songs you will not understand what I mean. To me, singing was a serious matter, to be done properly.

The times when my aunt, Mo, was here and there was a lot of laughter on TV she couldn't see anything to laugh about. "Noren ge khentan" (they are laughing again) she used to say with a poker face. English people do a lot of practical jokes, like a custard pie thrown to a face. And they all accept it as being amusing. While we, Armenians, call it "Eeshoo gadag" (donkey's prank). I, myself, hate practical jokes played on me - but wouldn't mind seeing somebody else being made a fool of.

Yet another observation of mine, is that we could be working with colleagues for many years and still call each other Miss, Mrs, or Mr. so and so. I was taken aback when my grandson's girlfriend, a music student like him, called me by my Christian name. She is just 20 years old and I am four times her age, and we haven't known each other very long. I don't think it is lack of respect, and yet, even at my age, I still address most people as Mr. or Mrs. If I didn't, there would be a few raised eyebrows as silent condemnation of familiarity. Are we taking this business of respect a little too far, maybe? We would never call a minister of ours by his name, and yet, in this country, they often say just "Tony Blair" when they are talking about the Prime Minister.

*   *   *   *

Over the years, I had the misfortune of losing a number of close friends and it fell on me to say a few last-minute words of tribute by the grave, as I did for Archbishop Bessak Toumayan and for Shaké Chakmakdjian. It was extremely hard to deliver those orations, because I was moved by the occasion and afraid of breaking down and not being able to continue. Poor Shaké, such a delicate creature with a tender heart and so many unfulfilled dreams. We can never forget her. As to Bessak Serpazan, he was a most accomplished clergyman and musician, with a wonderful trained voice, whose moving liturgy I am lucky enough to have on a recorded cassette. It gives me much pleasure to listen to it and makes me believe that I am right there, in God's domain. Poor man, he was made so unhappy, humiliated, disgraced and demoted as he was by the efforts of certain people who hated him for selfish reasons. He often paid us informal visits at home. We were his supporters to the end. He could speak to us openly about his disillusion. He wanted so much to regain people's respect. I said "Serpazan, when you die, even your enemies will come to your funeral to pay you their respects", and he replied with a childlike enthusiasm, "In that case, I am ready to go now!"

Yes, I was right. At his funeral the huge church of St. Peter's was absolutely packed, and yes, I saw there many of his tormentors who had come to see him off! Who can deny the fact that he was our first church leader ever to commemorate the anniversary of the genocide even against the orders of his employer Nubar Gulbenkian, who had just changed his nationality for personal reasons. Bessak Serpazan wasn't one of those who would forego his principles and crawl to people's whims in exchange of favours. He challenged Gulbenkian's authority, for which he was sacked from St. Sarkis Church. If only for the reason that he worked so hard towards the recognition of the Armenian Genocide, Bessak Serpazan deserved the respect of our community.

His successor, Bishop Nerses, became the darling of the community and also Pontifical Legate to the Catholicos. As soon as the new Ladies Committee of the recently acquired St. Peter's Church (granted by the Anglican authorities to Bessak Serpazan in the first place) was selected, he decorated his favourites with medals received on his recommendation from Etchmiadzine (our spiritual centre in Armenia). I was present at the ceremony during a banquet, where he singled out those women for that high honour when they had done absolutely nothing yet to deserve it - which was ridiculous. If this wasn't favouritism and flattery what was it? I can speak as a mature and experienced, hard working achiever with over fifty years of devoted service to my community under my belt, without any such recommendation. Since then, I have had the satisfaction of knowing that I am still active and have continued guiding the same group of ladies for over twenty years when all those decorated ladies have long since vanished from the scene like shooting stars.

I have carefully chosen my colleagues on the Ladies Committee from different organisations to work with me for the Armenian House. We also keep long-standing friendships alive with social gatherings and daytrips for all Armenian Ladies in our community. Recently we celebrated the 40th anniversary of the A.H. with guest singers and dancers. As long as I am able to continue in the service of my beloved Hai Doon, I will carry on with my hardworking committee. I was touched and gratified to see that they respected me enough to honour me on my 70th and 80th birthdays with surprise parties, in the presence of friends old and new. I used my initiative in organising events, receptions and trips and was the undisputed leader of our group. But the time had come for me to lighten my responsibilities and to nominate a successor to carry on the good work with all our support and encouragement.

In the many organisations I served, I left my mark. I contributed with my time and ability wholeheartedly. No one has ever been able to use me in pursuit of their own interests. I am, and remain, my own person. Had I put my name on a certain list of candidates during the Church Council elections in the eighties I would have gone on being elected again and again. I was approached delicately but I refused to toe the line. Fortunately the Armenian House is totally neutral and I know where I stand there.

So much has happened in this community in the last five decades that someone who has time, patience and ability, should undertake to write the history of London Armenians, chronologically and impartially. Anyway, that is not what I am trying to do, this is just my own private story with my own occasional observations. When, years ago, I used to send correspondence to Jamanak, I would keep going for several hours without stopping until I finished my article. I had better concentration and more fluency of thought then, and my pen would slide freely without restriction or stopping for inspiration, as is the case now. Now and again I refer to my old reports for some facts that should have been said before, hence the zigzagging back and forth.

CHAPTER 17 YET MORE MEMORIES

I have few relatives left in the world. Apart from my own immediate family and my brother's, there is Knar Chalikian in Los Angeles, who not only is my cousin from my grandmother's side, but also a childhood friend, who went to America and married very young. She has a son and daughter, and grandchildren. There is also Ovsanna Kaloustian in Marseille, a cousin from my grandfather's side. She is head of a large matriarchal family. I love both these women very dearly, we always correspond and give each other our news. We are all getting older by the day; who knows, will I be the one saying goodbye?

I have also got some dear friends in the States who came into our lives following a very strange dream. It was uncanny....We had just moved, from Wetherby Gardens to Cheniston Gardens at the end of December 1953. The Community Council's Christmas dance was on a Saturday night in January 1954, and when we managed to find a baby sitter, we decided to go. The next morning being Sunday we didn't mind getting up late. I was still in bed when I told my husband about the strange dream I had had. I had seen a young American Navy Officer in blue uniform, who gave me a parcel saying "this is for you". I will not mention what Krikor's sarcastic remark was here. As usual, it was always me seeing strange dreams. But that morning I just could not forget it.

Sometime later in the morning, when everybody was washed and dressed and fed, I busied myself in the kitchen preparing lunch, when the doorbell rang. Who could it be? We hadn't invited anyone. I went down to open the door. "You could have knocked me down with a feather" as the saying goes in English. It was an American officer in naval uniform with a parcel in his hands. I was standing there motionless as if I was stunned, gazing at his uniform, the blue blazer with gold buttons. His initially smiling face froze and he said "Is this Doctor Gorgodian's residence?"

Seeing how unwelcoming I was, he had thought that he was in the wrong place. He was young, charming and still standing there until I pulled myself together, apologised and asked him in. I called my husband down and we introduced ourselves. He could speak Armenian with a broad American accent, his name was Shant Haroutunian, and he was newly married to Louise. He had also just joined the U.S. Navy and was assigned to be based in London for two years. He was on his way to Church, but had a parcel for us from Mrs. Saraydarian, friends of his parents.

This lady was grateful to us because a few years before, her brother from Beirut had been sent to a hospital in London to have an operation to remove a brain tumour. We had been very helpful in arranging for him to see doctors, keep appointments, translate for him and even help him after the operation to travel back home. I think he got better and the whole family were grateful. I didn't know he had a sister in the States. Apparently he wrote and told her about us, and that's how Mrs. Saraydarian wished to express her thanks too.

We liked Shant very much and, meeting Louise later on, we became good friends with this young couple for the two years that they spent here in London. But that day when I dreamt that extraordinary and significant dream is so unforgettable. I remember how gratifying it was to see my husband eating humble pie. After all those years we have never stopped corresponding with Shant and Louise, at least at Christmas time, exchanging news and greetings. What a wonderful couple they were too, and blessed with two children, a girl and a boy. And now they are grand-parents.

I have had many such dreams but less dramatic than that one. I always had a notion that I might also be telepathic. I think I am sensitive to others' feelings towards me; I can tell whether they are sincere or not. It worries me when I have negative premonitions and I try to suppress them. Not all my dreams come true nor all my prayers. It may be very unconvincing but small miracles (as I call them) have resulted through deeply sincere prayers in dire circumstances. At such times the response has been immediate.

On one such occasion, during a Whitsun Bank Holiday, we were heading towards Great Yarmouth, driving in our dear old Hillman that had seen better days. When we reached the Colchester by-pass it was chockablock. We were stuck in the thickest traffic jam imaginable. Posh, powerful cars like Jaguars and Mercedes had their bonnets open, fuming on the hard shoulder. Surely we, with three children and suitcases packed in a little old car, hadn't a hope in hell. Our Hillman, like a spoilt family pet, had a mind of its own, which meant frequent stalling at the least provocation. Whenever we stopped at traffic lights we were not sure that it would start again. And now it had us all on tenterhooks. My husband was agonising and I was praying very hard. If the Hillman stopped, thousands of cars behind us would stay put. We needed a miracle very badly to make our little Minx keep going and let the traffic flow. The Colchester by-pass in the late sixties was the most dreaded narrow passage for motorists, just wide enough to let two cars scrape past each other. I think it was widened later on.

I prayed and prayed, my eyes tightly shut "Please God don't let it stall". In four hours of stop-start and crawl, we had covered just half a mile, leaving those powerful cars still fuming on the hard shoulder. Our little old Minx saw us through without a hitch. When eventually the road widened, I could see my husband wiping the perspiration from his face with a big sigh of relief. If that wasn't a miracle, then what was it? Though he claimed it was his mastery in driving that got us through! Men! Typical!

On another Bank Holiday, this time in August, we were motoring towards Devon and Cornwall, only then we had our shiny new Ford Corsair, which was automatic and more roomy. En route, we made an overnight stop at a motel, where we just managed to find accommodation. Once in Cornwall, we started our quest again beginning with the best hotels down to more modest places. Each time the answer was "sorry, we have no vacancies". We went round and round, up and down narrow streets, asking everywhere. And every time I was the one who had to do all the asking; Krikor wouldn't have known how to. I had had enough! "I am not budging anymore. Next time you do it!" One of the girls said jokingly "We could sleep in the car, that would be fun!" I took pity on him, he looked so worried and helpless. I started my conversations with God. "Please, please, help us dear God." It was hot and uncomfortable in the car. I said, "I want to stretch my legs a bit".

I got out and looked around. It didn't look like a tourist area at all, more like a residential back street with uneven buildings in a row. I saw a man polishing the brass door knob on the front door. I approached him hesitantly. "Do you have two rooms for the night?" He stopped what he was doing, "Which floor do you want?" I thought he was joking. "Can it be on the first floor, please?" He said, "Actually, we are not officially open yet, we are just putting the finishing touches. But you can come and have a look". I made a sign for the others to follow me. There was no lift, but never mind. It was a boarding house, clean enough, though not what we would have chosen had the situation been different.

It was recently refurbished, a modest but comfortable place. We took two rooms, clean, spacious, and airy, overlooking the garden. As we were the only guests, we got the best attention possible and stayed there to the end of our holiday.

We enjoyed our stay in Penzance with its views and restaurants, some with murals depicting heroics of legendary pirates, and of course their famous cream teas. A lovely place by the sea with palm trees and a more clement climate, and everyone was very friendly. By the end of our stay we had forgotten how difficult it had been to find accommodation, but I knew, it was through my prayers. God has listened to me many times in difficult circumstances.

Our summer holidays were always spent by the sea, a favourite choice. We did the length and breadth of the South Coast from Penzance right up to the Norfolk coast, and Jersey and Guernsey (where we visited Victor Hugo's house), yet we never went abroad all together. I have taken the girls to many of the islands in the Mediterranean: Majorca, Crete, Corfu, and also to the Côte d'Azure and Turkey. Later on they have travelled on their own to the world's interesting places. I, myself, do not like long journeys, especially in old age. I am an armchair traveller, and a keen watcher of travelogues.

When Mo and Daida, my aunt and uncle, had a flat in Paris, we all visited them at various times for long or short stays. We met their close friends in Paris, mother and daughter Kevorkians, and distant relative Shaké Hokdanian, who were a great help to them in later life. I was also pleased to be re-acquainted with Vartan Ozinian, formerly from Istanbul. Some time after my uncle's death when Mo was too old to manage alone, my brother arranged for her to move to a residential home. We sold the flat which was in a

163

very good location in the 16th Arrondissement with a heavy heart. We were very sorry to let it go, with all its memories.

We will never forget Mo and Daida. They were very dear to us, brother and sister, always bickering, but nevertheless living under the same roof for many years. They probably sacrificed their own private lives for each other. Neither of them had complete freedom of action. They needed each other for practical reasons and therefore resigned themselves to that situation. Daida died of a heart attack. He always smoked and drank too much; he had had a warning but did not care. When Mo was left alone, it was better for all our sakes and hers that she went to a home where she would be taken care of. She died a few years later as a result of a fatal fall, at the age of 101, still alert, but very frail.

I remember my maternal grandmother and grandfather from my childhood. My granny was the sweetest, kindest and most saintly woman I know. She had been a mother at 16 and Souren, her first born, was the apple of her eye. Mo, Daida and my mother were her other children. Souren was educated at the American college in Bardizag. I had never met him, he had died much earlier in New York. Souren had gone to the United States even before 1915. He was very artistic and very talented. He had a beautiful literary style, and always decorated his letters with flowers and birds and even wrote poetry. I liked corresponding with him, he was very witty too. Once he wrote to me, "Your letters are reminiscent of Madame de Sévigné" (who was renowned for her letter-writing). I took it as a compliment coming from him. His only souvenir is a violin of good quality, the one he carried with him when he left home in 1915, that was my grandmother's gift to him, and I have heard that it was quite expensive at the time, costing many gold sovereigns. He had no business acumen, never made much money, but never got rid of that precious violin that I later inherited and my grandson Daniel, a music student, is lucky enough to play now.

My mother was very artistic as well but in a different way. She had a very sweet singing voice and could still play the piano by ear so many years after the practice days of her girlhood. Mo too was very creative; she has made exquisite embroidery that I can't part with. They are like show pieces, too fragile to be used every day and not at all practical either.

My grandfather, Ghougas Miskdjian, was an entrepreneur. He was one of the first people to introduce running water not only to his own home, but he also built a fountain in his street to be used by the neighbourhood. Additionally, he had a hamam (Turkish Bath) built in his house that even relatives came to use. He was a shrewd self-made businessman who had a large store in Adapazar, where he sold novelty merchandise brought from Istanbul, sometimes imported goods from European countries, that no one else had seen before. He introduced the first Singer sewing machine and accordion and other interesting articles in his shop which, I was told, was like a mini-department store. He sold exotic materials and the Vogue catalogue, and my mother would choose herself a fashionable model, make her own pattern, and get some beautiful material from her father's store, like taffeta, silk or velvet, some imported from Vienna, and make an eye catching garment to dazzle the neighbours.

Their opulent house was visited by honourable guests, like visiting patriarchs and writers such as the poet, Alexander Panossian. My uncle Souren was the intellectual host to entertain them suitably.

When in 1915 they were all driven into exile, my mother was a new bride with a toddler, my brother Diran, and she used to wear all the nice clothes from her trousseau, since she hadn't any old ones. The peasants in Konya, where they were taken, used to harass her calling her names and saying things like, "You are rich, we will take everything you've got". And they did. My grandfather had abandoned everything, all his possessions, his residence, his business, and with the clothes they were wearing and a few bundles of necessities, the family was deported, not knowing where or for how long they were going. My grandfather had buried gold sovereigns in an earthenware pot in their garden with the hope of returning there one day, and they joined the group of deportees on their fateful journey to the dark corners of Anatolia.

Those unforgettable years. All their losses and suffering, during and after the deportation, and finally their escape to Istanbul, had caused enough nightmares. The family was left destitute and bitter. But they were lucky enough to come out alive after all the atrocities they endured.

*   *   *   *

Before my arrival in England, and after learning to speak French fluently at a French high school in Istanbul, I was surprised to discover that I had lost my confidence and fluency. When I went to Paris I was hesitant to make long conversations with the natives, I could just about manage short sentences. I couldn't remember the right words and it would take me a few days at least to find my feet, I was tongue tied. I did not think I could ever regain my previous proficiency.

I always loved the street markets in Paris, and when I visited Mo's flat, even when I didn't need anything, I used to go to the local marché in the 16th Arrondissement. I would walk up and down the aisles admiring the way they had arranged their fruits and vegetables so artistically, the colour co-ordination, reds with greens, blues with yellows. And even their fish counters, the fish so fresh, smelling almost of the sea, that you would think those creatures were still alive. And the shellfish, at least, were; I could see their tentacles moving. Every Sunday morning the stall holders would arrive early to set up their stalls and put up their shelves, and by 3 pm all would be sold and the frames would come down. In France it is common practice for most districts to have regular markets on given days. They are cheaper than the shops and probably sell fresher produce too.

I had the same difficulty speaking Turkish when I went to Istanbul some years ago. That was my birth place, where I lived 26 years before coming here to England. And yet, I couldn't remember ordinary words in everyday conversation. To make matters worse they had adopted new words I didn't know the meaning of. With lack of practice in French and Turkish over many years, my English had now overtaken those languages in which I used to be so proficient. I love the French language; if only the French didn't speak so fast.

For me, the most familiar place in Istanbul was Taksim Square and that's where our hotel was when my daughter Michèle and I last went six years ago. It was a huge modern building overlooking Atatürk's memorial. We were half way up on the seventh floor, and at night, when it was dark and all the lights in the square were on, I found the view magical. I would stand and stare out of the wall-to-wall windows of the modern hotel, with first-class accommodation and service by multilingual and courteous staff. It seemed to me that they had come a long way, those people, since the days I had left in 1946. Then everywhere on the buses and in public places, there were notices saying, "VATANDAŞ TÜRKÇE KONUŞ" which means "Speak Turkish Compatriots!"

How curious that they have changed their tune now. That notice was mostly for the non-Muslim minorities, like Greeks and Armenians and Jews. In modern Turkey they are trying very hard to live up to the European image, to put a foot in the door and pretend they are ready to enter the European Union. Their transformation is only superficial. Their women still cover their heads, and minorities remain vulnerable. Many young people are educated and multi-lingual, they are very polite to visitors from abroad and charming hosts. No wonder foreign visitors speak highly of them after they return home. They only see the polished façade of the tourist areas and not the back streets where the poor people live.

I had spent 26 years walking through Taksim Square every day, going to school or to work; I didn't live very far away. So now, nostalgia drove me to re-visit the place in which I had lived before I left in 1946. I knew the way, I knew exactly how to get there. My daughter and I started from the square going inwards through side streets, crooked, unpaved, dusty lanes. I stopped. That's where the House should be. I looked but did not recognise anything looking remotely familiar. Where was the House? It should have been here, but wasn't. My daughter said, "Are you sure this is the right street?" "Of course I am!"

All those houses, all those around that tiny spot, looked as if they were crumbling down and the pavement had levelled with the narrow street, and the whole area was like an excavation site.

Holes in the ground and rubble underfoot, like a disaster zone. I could imagine one downpour of torrential rain uprooting and washing everything away. It felt like being in a third world country. A languid Turkish song was blaring from the innards of those ruins as if coming from the other world, the world of ghosts.

And the most astonishing thing of all was not only that people lived in such a hole, but quite unbelievably, most had satellite dishes. My daughter couldn't believe her eyes: "How can they afford it?" Perhaps you don't have to pay for everything, if you know how.

I was still convinced this was the place I was looking for, and started looking for street names. There weren't any. Maybe the entire street was wiped off the map too. I had had enough, the nasty smell of blocked drains was lingering, in that stifling heat; utterly disappointed, I gave up my quest. "Let's go", I said, "I can't stand it, let's go."

We scrambled back from that inferno to the main road and in the distance, in all its glory, was our gorgeous hotel: The Marmara, standing proudly in Taksim Square, living testimony of civilisation. What a contrast! We went into the marble entrance hall where uniformed bell-boys were standing to attention. Up in the lift and to our beautifully modern suite with its marble bathroom and hostess bar for refreshments. I went to the window glancing in the direction of where we had just been, even the street wasn't visible. This was a different world altogether.

Apart from that, I recommend anyone going to Istanbul, to go and stay at the Marmara Hotel and enjoy the most fantastic breakfast you could find anywhere in the world and just help yourself! (One morning, we had an unexpected surprise when we bumped into

Levon Chilingirian in the dining-room, a fellow guest, who was invited to Istanbul to give a concert.) The clientèle is elite, mostly foreigners, and everything is absolutely first class. Unless, over time, the Marmara has lost its sparkle. There are other modern hotels all over Istanbul now. This is the most fascinating city between East and West, where the Bosphorus joins the Black Sea and the Marmara. All those mosques and palaces - some of them, like the Dolma Bahçe Sarayi (by architect Balian), the work of Armenian artisans and architects - and museums, and the Covered Bazaar. They have their own mystique and culture. Although the Turks are adopting European ways, their recent history is testimony of their Ottoman roots, and that is definitely the Orient.

In Istanbul, I managed to invite all my old school friends to afternoon tea at the Marmara Hotel. We had a very enjoyable time reminiscing. We were at school together in the mid-1930s, and had all changed since then. We tried to remember the old days, we didn't know then that they were special, we were all so young, in our teens, and the only cares we had were the exams. We had fantastic teachers, so dedicated, so thorough; they used to make sure that everybody understood the lecture. Not only were they excellent teachers but they were disciplinarians too. They inspired respect and they got it.

When I compare those days with the education system and the present day students, who can't even speak their own language properly, and are indifferent in class, rude, disrespectful, attacking their teachers physically, I wonder where things have gone wrong and how. Learning to respect your elders and betters starts at home. If children don't respect their parents they are not likely to respect anyone else. But obviously the parents' own attitude has a lot of influence on them. This is like the chicken and egg dispute. Maybe the parents too should know how to earn their children's respect. It has to start somewhere.

In my time, there was more than respect for teachers, there was awe and admiration that was to be remembered all your life. When my daughters went to Godolphin and Latymer school, they had highly qualified teachers who were in control of the class and were excellent educators. Even after finishing school, in all your life, you never forget your teachers, they have shaped your mind and built your character.

That afternoon in the Marmara Hotel, my old school friends and I talked about incidents that none of us had forgotten sixty years later. The school, the grounds, the gym, the chemistry lab, the stage and of course the headmaster and teachers. We all had some funny stories to tell. It made us feel young again, all of us old grannies!

They reminded me how I entertained the whole classroom during rainy lunch hours by mimicking the teachers, male and female. I used to ape their mannerisms and sing or talk like them. I used to chastise them mercilessly in my charades. My performance must have been true to life, because the girls used to fall about laughing. It was one such day that my act was cut short by a sudden warning of "shush!" My audience instantly froze. I was facing the girls, my back to the door; I couldn't see our form mistress peering through the glass panel on the top of the door. She walked in suspiciously and shouted, "What is going on?" As it happened, I was impersonating her, and she must have guessed. Seeing that she wasn't angry, somebody confessed to our having a little fun. She said, "At my expense too?" I couldn't answer, but my silence was admission enough. She threatened to punish me if I didn't "do" her. I said, "I can't". The girls shouted "Go on, you can". And I did. She laughed and laughed, and kept saying, "Do I really do that?" They all shouted, "Yes Miss". That was Oriort Azkanoush, who later became Mrs. Ghazarian, the owner of the Rivoli Hotel in Geneva.

Even though we had visited Istanbul before, Michèle and I still went sightseeing. Unfortunately we only had a week left, which we spent in Kuşadasi down the Aegean way by the sea, which was wonderful too.

Actually, the first time I returned to Istanbul was in 1971, 25 years after I had left it. We stayed at Baler Hotel, at a village called Ambarli nearer Küçukçekmece, with its own private beach by the sea. It was idyllic. The first day I went into the restaurant the head waiter served me with a smile and said, "So, you are now the loyal subjects of the Queen of England!". That was a very sarcastic remark, and I answered without hesitation, "Muhsin Bey, we, Armenians, are always loyal subjects wherever we live, as I myself was 25 years ago, and as all the Armenians still living here are now". We became friends, and he always gave us preferential treatment compared to the rest of the group, who were all tourists. In fact we liked it so much that two years later we went there again, my youngest daughter and I. It was right in the country with its beach, orchards and terraces.

Tension between us, Turks and Armenians, is rife now and I do hope it does not create an unbearable situation for those of us still living out there in Turkey, as I know by experience the kind of injustices their authorities are capable of inflicting on oppressed minorities. Let us hope we do not become a political pawn in the hands of powerful nations. Therefore, it is vital that we represent in the Diaspora a united front to the outside world.

CHAPTER 18 LAST MOVE

If I am not careful this isn't going to be just the story of my life but something like Scheherazade's Arabian Nights in which one story begets another for 1001 Arabian nights. I really would like to conclude this epic somehow if only I didn't keep remembering things.

It all started when I wanted to tell people how difficult it was for me to start a new life here. I always put it down to Providence for guiding me through thick and thin. It was written in my "djagadakir" (literally: letters written on your forehead, your fate) the way it was meant for me to meet my husband and live the kind of life we had together for thirty years: day and night never separated, his fatal illness and my despair after his death.

During all the heartache I went through, it only dawned on me later on how much he himself must have suffered not only physically but emotionally, seeing that life was oozing out of him drop by drop and he was going to be separated from his adoring family. One day, when I visited him in hospital, he just couldn't look at me, somehow avoiding my gaze. And when I said "why don't you look at me, I'll be going soon?" with his voice breaking, he said "I don't have to look at you to see you, your face is always in front of my eyes, day and night". How hard it must have been for him to know it would not be long for the death sentence to strike. Lying in bed helpless, his life ebbing away, until the last ounce was drained.

I wonder what it feels like to be in that situation. I do not know what kind of sentence awaits me. I hope it will be less painful for my children's sake. I would not wish to linger on aimlessly and keep everyone in suspense. The quicker the better towards the end and no regrets. I know I haven't been the perfect mother, but I only did what I could and thought was best, even if I was too strict. It was my way of protecting my children from likely pitfalls. It is too late to put the clock back now. Even if it were possible, there are certain situations I'd rather not be in again.

*   *   *   *

I had already been searching actively to move home when eventually I found a serious buyer for 29 Cheniston Gardens. I had three apartments to choose between and I was dithering. Time was short, I had to decide quickly. In the end I put down on paper "for" and "against", qualities and drawbacks, and by elimination I made my decision for the one in the backwaters of Barkers department store in Kensington, The Cottesmore Court. I needed three bedrooms in case any of the girls wished to stay until they were established elsewhere. After selling our family home with so many rooms and possessions I couldn't possibly fit in a pigeon hole just big enough for me. Michèle was in Australia but would be coming back soon, Anna was in Geneva, often visiting. Sonia was the only one in England with her own home and family, and she used to spend weekends here with her children.

The only disadvantage of the flat I chose was that it was not close enough to the High Street. But it was in a quiet residential area with five rooms and two bathrooms on the third floor, with a lift, suitable and adequate for us all.

My move from our large house was traumatic. It contained not only hundreds of memories but also much furniture, and belongings no longer required, and I spent many days deciding how to dispose of them. Some went to Bonhams auction rooms, some were given away. I had to bring the absolute minimum of essentials to fit in the flat. Over the years we had acquired a hoard of articles - I had no idea where they came from and how long they had been stuffed in the basement cupboards.

I put all my husband's army uniform, khaki shorts, shirts and boots in the big metal trunk he had brought back from Rangoon, with his name printed on it in big capital letters "CAPTAIN K GORGODIAN", and reluctantly gave it to the Red Cross to take away. Other papers, letters, photos, medals are with me for safe keeping. The rest of the paraphernalia took some time to dispose of.

I felt wretched to be parted from many things, even useless hoards that reminded me of some of my beloved departeds. I had to tear myself away from some articles, fixtures and fittings that were immovable, like the beautiful Italian black marble fireplace in the waiting room, the white marble ornamental one in the living room, both exquisite. The big bulky brass curtain rails, the mahogany elegant banister running down all the way from the top floor and the pretty stained glass panels enhancing the front door, and the ornately patterned mosaic floor in the entrance hall.

I hope whoever inherited those treasures will appreciate not only their beauty but also the antique value of their new and unique acquisitions. The lucky buyer, an Armenian from Damascus squeezed a hard bargain, taking advantage of my desperate wish for a quick transaction. He wasn't going to live there himself, he had the house converted into six flats and sold them individually, making a bomb.

Nowadays, when I pass that corner going to the Armenian House, it is heart breaking to see our old house in such a neglected and run-down condition. It doesn't look remotely like my beautiful homely "Gorgodian Palace" that once housed a happy large family oozing life and activity. Today, the windows and curtains are filthy, the black garbage bags spill open on the pavement and the whole place is in a pitiful condition. I am glad my husband is not around to see that pathetic sight.

I am well established in my compact cosy flat, even if it could do with updating after all these years. My next-door neighbour and I, both elderly, keep a watchful eye on each other. Mrs. Margot Curran is a much travelled and knowledgeable lady and a very interesting conversationalist. The area is very select and security is tight in our block. I wish my beloved husband were here with me to enjoy the comfort and amenities a well run flat can offer, even if it costs the earth to maintain it.

The whirlwind of activities have stopped for me for sometime now. I prefer the slow lane, near the hard shoulder, where occasionally I can stop to recharge my batteries. I move in slow motion: slow in everything. I try to keep from over-exerting myself for everybody's sake. No more parties and outings unless I am taken. I still attend meetings for the A.H. only. The telephone is my lifeline and thanks to my close friends I make full use of it. I also watch television discriminately, documentaries and good films, but not too many or late at night. I am not interested in sports but I do get excited when an Armenian athlete breaks a record in championships, when Aghassi wins, or even some of the new names in tennis, like Nalbandian from Argentina, Sarkissian from Armenia, and the teenage girl from Geneva, Gayané Mikaelian. I even like Cher, because she is Sarkissian. And I read that Jean Simmons was half-Armenian, Vivian Leigh had Armenian blood, and so did Diana, the Princess of Wales. I had always loved her anyway, and the whole world knows her true story. I don't blame her for her wrongdoings, she was driven by desperation, she would have behaved differently herself if she were a happy wife in the first place.

A year after her wedding I took a 57 seater coach load of ladies to Althorpe, her ancestral home. She wasn't there of course, but it was very interesting to see where the new Princess of Wales was brought up. Since she died we have made three more journeys to Althorpe, to pay our respects to that lovely girl's memory. Her brother, the Earl Spencer, was welcoming visitors in his rolled up shirt sleeves, tall and handsome, nothing haughty about him, a very charming man. All the net proceeds of the takings are donated to her memorial fund. We were filled with awe at her museum and at the lake where she now rests in peace on a small island.

CHAPTER 19 CONCLUDING NEWS & VIEWS

It takes a crisis to make us realise where our priorities lie. It is never too late to make amends. I have often tried to keep the peace in adversity. I always forgive people whenever they apologise, though it is not that easy to forget. But some people's egos are too big to admit they are wrong. Fortunately I have quite a few friends who have known me for a very long time and there is no pretence between us. We pay regular visits by telephone. Mimi Bacon and I are very close indeed, we know what goes on in each other's lives. Sima Kahve, Santin Hougassian and I also talk often. Peggy Shishmanian is my oldest friend, Ojik Brose a later addition. Rita Cherchian (also from Istanbul) calls me when she is not in Timbuktu or Siberia, or some other unearthly place, like on scaffolding, or on the motorway doing 120 miles an hour. I am afraid I am not going to be able to name everyone I know, but I mustn't forget some very dear friends I may not meet frequently but who are often in my thoughts. Joyce in Madrid, and in London: Ani Tchelbakian, Dicky Darzi, Vehanoush and Hasmig Gulvanessian, Armineh Carapeti, Veron Kaprielian, Berjouhi Gosdanian, Rosie Gregory, Shoushanig Kalfayan, Shoghig and Parkouhi Minassian, Dikranouhi Healey, Princess Helena Moutafian, Silva Yeghiazarian, Hayguhi Aivazian, the daughters of my dearest friend the late Hayguhi Ghazarian, Christine and Marie, Sirvart Artan and Ophelia who went to the States. There are many more whose names I cannot recollect right now, and all those nice people I used to like so much but who are no longer with us. I think I have more friends who are spirits now than of this world. What a grand party we will hold over there when I go to join them some time in the distant future. I hope not yet, I still have quite a lot of loose ends to tie up.

On the whole we have quite a nice community here, and a good many organisations which are all doing their bit to carry the torch, like:

The Community and the Church Council, the Hayastan All Armenian Fund, the AGBU, CAIA, The Armenian Institute, Anahid Association, Nor Serount Cultural Association, HOM, the Sunday and Saturday Schools, Navasart Cultural Association, Hamazkayin, our two Churches, Manoukian Cultural Foundation, and definitely our beloved Hai Doon. Forgive me if I have forgotten any others. This is a formidable list of cultural bodies for a small Nation's small community.

It was an unforgettable experience for me to visit "The Ark" exhibition at the British Library in 2001. I was overwhelmed with emotion, a fantastic feeling of pride and delight at this public demonstration and proof of our national culture, and an ancient civilisation that dates back to Noah's Ark. Our heartfelt thanks to Vaché Manoukian who initiated and produced that outstanding show. Hats off to him for also returning to us our old, draughty, cold and uninviting church in such a magnificent transformation. If only he would let us have an annexe for the congregation to meet after service over a cup of tea, to feel the togetherness we miss so much! I do hope someone will give him this heartfelt message. God bless him and his family anyway.

As I write these lines, it is winter of 2002 now, and in the winter of my life I have time to stop and think. On reflection, I had a full and happy life after getting married. I was never idle or bored. Even in the earlier days of my life, from the moment I left school, I had a job that made it possible for me to provide for my parents until I came to England. I went through some very hard times that I managed to overcome by the grace of God. I try not to remember those dark days.

Since writing my memoirs, so many incidents that lay buried surfaced one by one, so much so, that I was bewildered and lost my sense of continuity. Not everything is worth mentioning. Some may be boring, and more importantly, utterly confidential. Furthermore, this is not a confessional, and at times I may have said more than I ought to have done. Also, I occasionally diverged into personal thoughts and convictions, like beliefs in the occult, reincarnation and the Law of Karma. Those are doctrines that I tried to study by correspondence after I left school. Later on when my life became more complicated, there was no time for meditation and contemplation. I just could not concentrate when I had so much to do.

In fact I have kept a congratulatory letter from Alice Bailey, that distinguished and eminent author on cosmic science, to urge me not to abandon my studies. I was invited to the symposium of the Arcane School in 1951 in Tunbridge Wells and met her personally. I was given her highly specialised book on the subject that was well above my grasp then, and even more incomprehensible now. I read a few pages of it now and again without much understanding, but fascinated by the subject all the same. The hardback book is 650 pages long and the title is "Treatise on White Magic". (By the way, it has nothing to do with magic as we know it.) I regret giving up my course. It is such an absorbing subject.

Looking back, some of my actions may seem adventurous or daring, considering my limited experience in life; my stunted education and the stifling and confined environment in which I spent my formative years. I count myself lucky and privileged to have sailed through those dark days, as I always acknowledged with the help and guidance of Providence. Married life brought maturity and wisdom, thanks to the continuous support of my husband, who was so much older than me, had seen the world and lived a life abroad in the army. He was my guru, and I became more tolerant in carrying out my responsibilities in the community at large.

One of the things my husband also taught me was humility, understanding and seeing the other side of the coin. We become so wrapped up in our problems that we ignore others' concerns. I know I am not perfect, and I can only try. The only things I cannot tolerate are injustice and spite. When I was left alone and had to make my own decisions, I became gradually more daring after a period of losing self confidence, and gathered the necessary strength to face life alone. When you have lost your better half, you are left with less than half your aptitudes; you are also standing alone on the social circuit. I immersed myself more and more in developing my existing social programmes, always considering new projects for our Ladies coffee mornings.

When I read in the Woman magazine that they were offering make-overs for clubs, I remembered my own experience in 1949 and wrote to them inviting them to the A.H. for a demonstration. The reply was a "change of plan". They said that they would now only accept individuals at the magazine's own premises, and invited me to attend. This would be a new feature for the over 70s, and I think I was the oldest to participate.

I accepted their invitation after consulting Mimi. First, I had to fill in a questionnaire, then go to a separate cubicle to have my face done and my hair washed and set, choose the clothes that suited me from an assortment of dresses on a rail, all new merchandise from clothing firms. They offered coffee and sandwiches while waiting. The transformation took a couple of hours, then the photographic session started. We were called one by one for different poses, either sitting or standing. When it was all done they promised to send us an issue of the magazine and copies of the photos taken. It was such a unique experience. Fortunately, my friend Mimi was with me as I thought I wouldn't have the courage to go it alone. The following week, I received my copy and the photos, which were rather flattering. Suddenly I had an attack of panic. "Qu'en dira-t-on?", what will people say?

I hadn't told anyone, but it couldn't be kept a secret. A few Armenian ladies who bought the "Woman" and saw me on those pages started spreading the news. As I suspected, the calls kept coming in. "How did you get in the magazine? How did you manage it? Did you know anyone inside? Did they pay you?" I had to tell them how it all happened, and make it look unimportant - after all I was fully dressed and nothing was suggestive! And, NO, I did not get paid, I did not do it for money. Mimi being there the whole time confirmed that all was above board. After a while the curiosity died down. One thing that bothered me in all this was that in their description of me by the photos, along with some personal details on this "stunning granny" it was mentioned that I "came from Armenia". In the questionnaire I had to fill in, I put myself down as a "British Armenian" in order to avoid saying I came from Turkey, in case they labelled me as "Turkish". It is very difficult for English people to understand that you may have been born in China but that doesn't make you Chinese.

How many stories do I need to write to make this book look like "The Tales of the Arabian Nights"? I think there were 1001 tales, one for each night if I am not mistaken. Although I have the book I never read the whole thing through. I attempted a few times but never had the patience to finish and I am wondering now what happened to Scheherazade in the end. Did she manage to keep her head? Fortunately there aren't so many chapters in mine. I doubt if her stories had anything to do with ordinary people, poverty, ageing, sickness, life and death. You must need a vivid imagination and spirit of adventure to initiate such an extravagant fantasy into a legend of that magnitude. A never-ending narrative that excites your curiosity so much so that you cannot put the book down until all the mystery is unravelled. Well, I did put the book down. I lost my patience.

I can assure the reader that my own story has nothing to do with imagination or fiction. It is based on true experiences, not terribly exciting nor fascinating. It may be banal, an everyday story of ordinary folk, but it is not fabrication. You may only want to read it because you know the writer, and are curious about her private life. Whoever you are, I hope that you enjoy reading the accounts of a former unintentional asylum seeker and see how difficult it is to adapt to new ways and cultures without knowing the language, or having a job and money. I have no regrets starting my story. It was an experience worth going through, remembering the good and the bad times, but I wouldn't like to live my life all over again. Past mistakes cannot be corrected, you can only learn from them.

In all my life I never lost my faith in God, rather, my reverence for God. I have such a sensitive conscience that I always know when I am in the wrong and subsequently await retribution. If I don't get it in this life, I will suffer for it in the next. I was initiated in the belief of reincarnation years ago in my youth and found it very believable. Most people would argue that there is no concrete evidence, unless they are interested enough to study the subject thoroughly and form their own opinion.

I read a very interesting article once where it says that manuscripts have been found in India "relating to the voyage of one man called Issa, who came from Bethlehem to study in the Tibetan cloisters the secrets of the occult with the Masters, and several years later, he returned to preach to his people; but in Palestine, he was condemned to death by Pontius Pilate". This script coincides with reality, and suggests that Jesus was that man from Bethlehem. In the Bible, there is no account of his activities after his adolescence until his 30s. What was He doing between those years? Perhaps the manuscripts about Issa provide the missing link. A man with Christ's status wouldn't disappear from the scene silently. He wouldn't busy himself in a shed only cutting wood, or quietly minding his own business like an ordinary and insignificant person. He, Jesus, would mingle with the crowds, He would be in the temple rubbing shoulders with the worshippers or would be arguing with the rabbis, He would moralise and rebuke people for wrongdoings. He would not be a silent figure for ten years or more. He would also be doing a few miracles on the side. The question of his actions through adolescence and beyond needs clarification either by religious leaders or historians. To me this mystery is more important than a fossil found 5 million years ago. All races believe that Jesus existed. He was the greatest prophet in the world, and some of us believe, the Son of God. For over 2000 years, we are still celebrating his birth and death.

People are always curious to find out more about their origins. I normally watch on TV anything to do with our past, whether historical or prehistoric. The most amazing artefacts are found in excavations in South America, in Egypt, in Turkey and in Asia. After all this time they still haven't found the relics of Noah's Ark, because they are looking in the wrong places, such as the bottom of the Black Sea or in Mesopotamia.

Fossils, caves, shipwrecks, lost civilisations always attract attention. At least those searches are done in places still accessible to man. I wonder if there are any lost worlds in the universe? Even if they are discovered, by the time their messages reach us after so many light years, our civilisations may have ceased to exist. And yet, man is curious to find his origins whether it be celestial or terrestrial.

In the meantime the population in the world is multiplying uncontrollably. We call the poorest of the poor in Africa the third world, and tons of food are sent there by the UN. Those uneducated simple people are not in control of their own lives. Their animal instinct is reproduction, and whether they are wasting away or have some deadly disease, like AIDS, they are unable to check the situation. They produce baby after baby while malnutrition is rife, hanging above their heads. Sending them food is not the answer, at least, not the only one. Those people should be taught to stop producing sickly children that become a burden on the world at large. I do not condone what the Chinese are doing in their own country, but at least they took the initiative of restricting multiple births by putting a limit of one child per couple. They are a clever race and they want to be self sufficient.

How fortunate we are that most of us have roofs over our heads and have healthy families. Of course there is no guarantee to safeguard anything in this world, but we have some control of our lives. We raise our children to the best of our abilities and they in their turn follow the pattern. At the ripe old age of 82, I was doubly blessed very recently by becoming a great grandmother to my granddaughter's new born baby boy. Georgia married Martin last year, a lovely, hard working, intelligent young Englishman, and it makes me very happy to see how blissfully contented they are in their own home. I never knew I would live to see another baby in our family. I give thanks to God and ask for his blessing on all my children and theirs. I hope that when my end is near, I will not linger aimlessly, to spare my daughters unnecessary grief.

*   *   *   *

As I type these lines the New Year has just started and I do hope 2003 will be a better one than the last, for the sake of the whole world, as the danger of war is looming on the horizon, explosive bombs and killer chemical warfare are threatening the peace in many countries. I remember many years ago, a very odd looking man in Oxford Street, with a big life-size wooden cross strapped to his back, who used to carry a banner with large handwritten print saying "THE END OF THE WORLD IS NIGH"; well, here we still are 40 years later. I wonder is he is still around? Maybe that message is more appropriate now and he should seek a wider audience.

I have heard some old people say that "We are in the departure lounge" when they are joking about death and not taking it seriously. I think it may actually be true. Nowadays, with all the strikes going on, whether air traffic controllers or seamen or railmen, the departure lounges are full of would-be passengers waiting miserably for their delayed transport, spending the night sleeping bent over their luggage, and wasting uncertain hours checking time tables. Fed up and edgy, they are using their holiday spending money in the departure lounge. It is never comfortable in the departure lounge, you never know when your transport will turn up. In my case, I am not yet ready and packed. I haven't made any arrangements, I have still got a lot to do, and when I go to my departure lounge, I want my carriage to be on time. I do not want to wait long, just to have enough time to say good bye to my family who will come to see me off at a painless departure. I have had enough pain these last years to compensate for some of my wrongdoings, or retribution, or part payment towards my Karma. I cannot say my slate is absolutely clean but it can be wiped clean, given time.

The reader may think that I am a simple person. That would be right. I have kept some of my childlike innocence and naiveté. I trust and believe in people. When I was around eight years old, a girl in my class who was much older than me (our classes were not age-related as they are now and I was the youngest in the class) said "This year Easter is going to be on a Sunday". I went home to announce the news only to be told that it always falls on a Sunday. Through life I have tended to trust people most of the time. Even though life experience has taught me to see through them, I still give them the benefit of the doubt, mainly, I think, because my husband advised me not to judge people. He wasn't always right. But then, who is?

I started writing this book of my memoirs, and along the way, I have added a narrative of my beliefs and observations. I am an unknown writer, an obscure person with an obscure story, full of repetitions. No-one outside the Armenian Community has ever heard my name; why should anyone be interested in my memoirs? My style is unproven and unsophisticated. I am not overly hopeful or ambitious. There is no mystery, crime, horror or sex involved in my story. It is all down-to-earth, about everyday things that most people go through. Simplicity is my motto, not only in my writings, but in my lifestyle as well. All I want is to have this book published so that my family will remember past things about their father and mother and be proud of them. I have mentioned little about their own lives, that is not my business, nor anyone else's.

I have often wondered what incentive people have to do good in life. What motivates them? A moral code? Faith in God or something else? We all know about Mother Theresa, goodness personified. But recent revelations about her religious doubts may have influenced many people's faith in God. She was an inspiration and a role model to even Diana, the Princess of Wales, who looked up to her in admiration and felt encouragement in her charity work. Mother Theresa must have been overwhelmed with the misery surrounding her. But if she had believed in the law of Karma, she would have realised that all the sufferings she witnessed were not without a purpose.

Once an agnostic philosopher declared on his deathbed: "If there is a watch there must also be a watchmaker". I believe the whole universe is not just an accident as a result of the big bang. Where did it all start? How can we measure time in infinity? Everything in the universe is calculated and works like clockwork, it is all too awesome, too miraculous for simple inquisitive minds like mine. Astronomers keep discovering new stars and give them names. What puzzles me is that all the stars and planets in the galaxy are globular. Is it because they are revolving all the time or the other way round? The universe is so complex it will take mankind several reincanations to penetrate its mysteries. Step by step, with intelligent perseverance man will get there in the end. But it will be with God's will.

Meditation, contemplation, yoga, astral bodies, the laws of Karma, reincarnation are part of studies into cosmic science, which may seem unattainable now or even incredible for most people, but volumes have been written on the subjects. It is not all imagination, there may not be concrete proof for the doubting Thomas's, and most of us are. According to the Law of Karma, we do not just get marked down for our trespasses, we also get recognition for our good deeds and thoughts.

What I found in the Roman Catholic faith is that during a confessional, people repent their sins by their thoughts, words, deeds and by "omission". This last condition has no part in the teaching of our own church. The priest recites all the mentionable and unmentionable sins we may have been guilty of doing in the confessional, but "omission" is the clause that doesn't appear in his list. You may have done nothing but good in your life, but if you also failed to do good when you could or should have done, that is a sin as well. Do we think that after communion we become better people? Maybe after an initial restraint we continue just as before. The road to hell is paved with good intentions, they say.

Lent is a good excuse for repenting. Self control and sacrifices, denial of the things you like to eat or do. Throughout my youth, for years, I was submitted to Lent unwittingly. It wasn't a self imposed denial when we didn't eat meat or good food. My Lent wasn't just for forty days, it was for many years. It was a way of life. We couldn't afford the good things. My mother was very good at making ends meet, making a little go a long way, using the cheaper cuts, buying produce at reduced prices, stretching our meagre budget and trying not to have debts. She was an expert at all that; considering that she came from a wealthy family, I wonder how she learnt that skill. I suppose it was a case of having to.

I have inherited my mother's knack in that way by just watching her and learning. I knew how much I earned and what our budget was. Dire circumstances make you very adaptable in life. I have emerged a stronger person as a result. On reflection, all my life's work regarding my family and my commitment in community affairs are a labour of love. There have been many turning points, sharp reversals and desperate measures. In fairness, those hazards are put in your path as trials. It depends how you deal with them. There are times when you despair and give up the struggle, and yet again, a driving force makes you sit up and take courage to continue.

Wouldn't it be nice if time stood still and I, not a day older, doing the same things without worrying about tomorrow? Not having to do soul destroying things I hate or dislike or moan about, like tidying, ironing, kitchen chores, washing, drying and having difficult, fussy guests? What about bills? Do I have to pay? I would stop the clock if I could, yet would I still have my ongoing pains, my bad sight, arthritis, troublesome hip and aching feet? Would they also give me, if time stood still, the patience I need to please everyone, the strength I need to walk everywhere, the stomach I need to digest everything, the humour I need to dispel my woes, all the love I need to forgive my foes? Be polite to bores and pretend I enjoy their presence? And, would things get better or worse tomorrow?

If you are young you have hope, if you're past sixty or seventy or in my case eighty, you cannot expect things to get better. Be thankful if you can stand still for a long time. But, what was that I learnt to say "every day in every way I am getting better and better" or something like that? If that isn't self-deception what is it? Every morning when I get up, I check to see if I can remember what happened yesterday or even last night. Then I start the new day, and ask myself, what is the next move? Can I follow the routine, all those mundane things in the bathroom, kitchen, bedroom? My "must do" notes for the day on my desk need my attention. The Daily Telegraph crossword is my mental exercise that makes my brain work. Do I remember my prayers to start my morning, not parrot fashion but knowingly, meaning every word? When I was in French school, I said to Sister Marthe one day "Ma soeur, some nights, when I say my prayers in bed, I fall asleep in the middle" and she said to me "Mon enfant, God knows what you were going to say next and that is in your subconscious, it continues without you realising it and God accepts that".

It was reassuring to know that He was there for me, and I have had that manifestation many times in my life. I call them my "small miracles".

Life is too short they say. That is true of one life, when we are supposed to be preparing the ground for the next life, and the next, until we reach the point of culmination.

It will take countless generations for science and religion to merge in infinity and then we can find God, just as Christ did in his last incarnation: He had finally accomplished his mission as the Messiah.

WE HAVE A VERY LONG WAY TO GO YET